Findir
Principles fo

FINDING THE HEART
PRINCIPLES FOR TAI CHI AND LIFE

Alfons and Ulrike Staerk
www.KeruUmaBudo.com

Third Edition

About This Book

The following book is a reflection of thoughts, class teachings and learnings through our martial arts journey.

Those reflections have also been published on our blog: KeruUmaBudo.Wordpress.com but have been edited and adapted for this book to present a more structured and logical flow.

Additional updates, announcements, videos, and pictures are always posted on our website: KeruUmaBudo.com.

Pictures and illustrations are either copyright of Alfons and Ulrike Staerk or shared under Creative Commons CC0 from Pixabay.

Copyright

First Printing: 2018

ISBN 9781724173683

Keru Uma Budo
Carnation, WA 98014
www.KeruUmaBudo.com

To our teacher Hilmar Fuchs who patiently showed us the path.

To our parents who provided the resources and encouragement to follow the path.

To our students who embarked on the journey with us and enabled us to understand the art on a deeper level.

To our kids who have to deal with their strange parents.

CONTENTS

Introduction 1

  Foreword 2

  Preface 4

  Keru Uma Budo 7

Part I Keep The Art Alive 11

  Shu Ha Ri – How we learn 12

  About Preservers and Creators 14

  Famous Teachers and the 'True Form' 17

  Why Aren't More People Practicing Tai Chi? 18

  Learn From Heart to Heart 20

Part II Principles Of Movement 25

  Don't Break Your Knees! 26

  Focus On Your Eight Points 29

  Cut the Strings 31

  Open and Close 33

  Empty and Full 35

  Tuck in Your Tailbone 37

  Work Against Resistance 39

  Open your Lao Ghong and Yong Quan Points 41

  It All Starts With Your Feet 43

Pay Attention to Your Eyes...46

Yin and Yang – Keep Flowing..49

Qi follows Yi..53

Spiral Energy...56

Part III Augment Your Learning 61

Take Notes 62

The Form Is Just A Container...64

The Answer Lies in The Small Details...65

Make as Many Mistakes as Possible!...69

The Power of Metaphors 73

Let Your Imagination Soar 75

Let's Go Flying...77

How Would Your Spirit Animal Do The Form? 79

Remember the Feeling, not the Explanation 84

Learn and Forget...86

Have Fun and Enjoy the Ride!...88

Part IV Tai Chi For Health 91

The Three Legs of a Stool...92

Stretch Gently...96

Loosen Your Joints 98

Strengthen Your Core...100

Improve Your Balance 102

Train Your Brain 105

Learn To Be In The Moment...106

Your Posture Defines Your Mindset 107

Improve Your Sensitivity and Awareness 110

Go Outside 113

You Are Never Too Old..115

Part V Reflections On Martial Arts and Life 119

Slow is Smooth, Smooth is Fast 120

No Ranks, No Titles..123

How Many Different Arts Should You Explore? 125

Like Climbing a Mountain 128

The Lifelong Apprentice Mindset 131

On Martial Arts and Business 134

To Those Who Have Forgotten More Than We Will Ever Learn.....141

Our Teachers 142

Important Influences..145

The Path Ahead..146

Appendices..149

Tai Chi Principles..150

Important Acupuncture Points..152

Form of 24 154

Form of 103 – Yang Form 157

Book Recommendations..166

INTRODUCTION

"To find and to understand the principles means
to find the heart."
Hilmar Fuchs

FOREWORD

I t is an honor to be asked to write a foreword for a book and demonstrates that the authors put great trust in you. It is a great pleasure for us to see this book come together after the many years and countless hours of training we spent together. Uli and Alfons went through the stages of imitation, reflection and then venturing out for their own way (Shu, Ha, and Ri). In this book, they are passing on the experiences they made on their way to their students.

The student who truly tries to understand an art will embark on a journey to discover what lies behind the pure technical execution of the movements. At some point, the student will feel the essence behind the art. This new awareness will transform her personality, which will now be in harmony with nature.

In the western cultures, we often look at martial arts more as a form of acrobatics. Few people look at what is behind the outer shell. To find and to understand the principles (the essence) means to find the heart. Furthermore, those principles are the basis for a life of morality, humanity, justice, acceptance, and wisdom.

This book tries to offer those principles as a foundation for the student who embarks on the journey to discover the art on a deeper layer. Understanding the essence will provide a solid foundation to further develop the technical movements of the art of Tai Chi.

At some point in our journey, we stumbled upon this proverb:

"A picture is worth a thousand words!"

A picture helps us to express our emotions and thoughts and also to compare them with our path through life.

This picture reminds me how we start with shared roots. We develop and grow together from those strong roots. When we are ready, we start to branch off into our own independence and find our own path without forgetting the roots that connect us.

Alfons and Uli have found their path and shared their personal emotions, sensations and thoughts in this well-written book.

To find the principles (the essence) means to find the heart.

Marlene and Hilmar Fuchs
www.mh-health.com
Cape Coral, FL, 2018

PREFACE

U li and I have been practicing various forms of martial arts for over 25 years. We learned Karate, Kobudo and Tai Chi from our teacher Hilmar Fuchs. We studied Aikido for a while with a friend. We explored Jodo with one of the leading experts in North America. We spent some time learning the Yang family style teachings in the school of a direct decedent of the Yang family and current leader of the style. We learned how defensive shooting techniques and empty hand fighting can be combined into a coherent system.

In my day job, I studied Physics and learned the importance and effectiveness of understanding first principles and describing the world from there. At the same time, I worked high responsibility and high-stress executive leadership jobs at Microsoft and Amazon for almost as long as I studied martial arts, making it critical for me to understand the balance and flow between focus and relaxation.

Uli is a Medical doctor and by trade has always been very focused on healthy living and nurturing our bodies and minds. She also worked in high-stress environments and has painful firsthand experience as to what that can do to your wellbeing.

All of these experiences come together in this book. We did not want to write a book about how to perform a specific technique or form in a specific style. Rather we wanted to talk about and explain underlying principles that hold true across styles and will lead you, so we hope, to deeper understanding and a richer path through your martial arts journey.

Most of the principles and thoughts in this book come from what we have learned over the years from our teacher Hilmar Fuchs. Some were inspired by other leaders in martial arts and outside of that realm. And yet another set was driven and inspired by questions from students in our classes. Occasionally we had some insights on our own.

My spirit animal is the horse, which, together with the love of Uli and

our daughter for horses, inspired the name of our school, Kicking Horse Tai Chi (Keru Uma Budo). It also reflects my need for freedom and finding my own way, which you can probably spot in a few of the thoughts and recommendations we're giving. We truly believe that you need to develop strong roots but then find your own way.

Uli's spirit animal is the mouse. Like a mouse, she is curious and looks into all corners of a problem to come back up with an unexpected insight that she found. Like a mouse, she also likes to be grounded and stay out of the limelight. Uli is a passionate artist and art teacher at our kid's school.

Being a visual person, she loves using imagination and pictures to support her teaching. Look for her thoughts on visualization and imagination throughout this book.

With that, we hope you will enjoy the book, find a few things that make sense to you and maybe enrich your own practice. We cannot teach universal truths, but we aim to offer ideas for your own explorations.

Have fun, practice, reflect and enjoy every day!

Alfons
Carnation, WA, 2018

KERU UMA BUDO

Keru Uma Budo – kicking horse martial arts – symbolizes the life philosophy we adopted after 25 years of practicing and teaching budo (martial arts).

Like a wild horse, enjoy life and your freedom, roaming green pastures under wide open skies. Build affectionate relations and friendships. Be compassionate. Have fun. There is no limit to what you can do.

However, you never want to get in the way when a kicking horse feels that it needs to defend itself or its family.

ALFONS STAERK

Alfons has been practicing Tai Chi, Karate, Kobudo and other martial arts since 1992 and holds a 4th-degree black belt in Karate (awarded in 2005; he received his 1st-degree black belt 1996). He has been giving classes for all age groups since 1993 with a special focus on self-defense as well as health aspects.

Alfons received his Karate instructor and examiner licenses from the German Olympic Sports Confederation in 2004 and his Tai Chi instructor license for Komatsu-Ha 2009 in Florida.

Professionally Alfons is a senior technology manager at Fortune 500 companies (including Amazon and Microsoft) and passionate people coach.

ULRIKE STAERK

Uli started Tai Chi, Karate, and Kobudo in 1993 and holds a 3rd-degree black belt in Karate (awarded in 2006; she received her 1st-degree black belt 1999). She has been giving classes for all age groups since 1997. Uli has a strong interest in holistic health and wellbeing, combining exercise, nutrition, and the arts.

She received her Karate instructor and examiner licenses from the German Olympic Sports Confederation in 2004 and her Tai Chi instructor license for Komatsu-Ha 2009 in Florida. In 2016 she was awarded a Yonkyu Shihan teacher diploma by the Sogetsu School in Tokyo, Japan.

Uli is a Tai Chi and Ikebana teacher and art docent at her kid's school. She was a Medical Doctor in Germany, practicing at the University of Aachen and others, before focusing on raising her two kids. These days she is also busy as the lead art docent at her children's school.

PART I
KEEP THE ART ALIVE

"When children are young, give them roots. When they get older, give them wings."
Hilmar Fuchs

SHU HA RI – HOW WE LEARN

Teaching and learning in traditional martial arts are divided into three phases: Shu (obey), Ha (detach) and Ri (leave). Over the years of studying the art, a student moves through those phases until she finds her own way. Don't try to hasten to Ri too quickly, it takes decades. Trying to find shortcuts will distract and confuse rather than help the progress.

Shu – This is the phase that every student in every martial art starts with. The purpose is to exactly follow the teacher's instruction and precisely copy her. During this phase, the body will learn the movements and sub-consciously get a 'feel' for the principles at play.

Ha – After years of practice, a student will more deeply understand the principles that are lying behind a martial art and its techniques. She will understand what's critical for the art and what's just an expression of style from different teachers. The student will start to learn what interpretation and variation will work best for her body. This is the time when students start to experiment with the art and slowly and carefully go beyond the boundaries of what they are presented with in class.

Ri – After decades of practice, the student's body will have learned the principles of the movements. It will have become a natural part of her body. The student will have discovered what works best within the special abilities and constraints of her body as well as what works best for others that she teaches. It is now time to find her own interpretation, to develop the art further and contribute to keeping it adapting and alive. The student will leave the teacher to find her own way, although she will never lose the connection to her roots or her teacher. Even in Ri, a student is not finished learning. She will seek out other masters and other arts to broaden her understanding and bring new ideas back to her art.

ABOUT PRESERVERS AND CREATORS

Over the years I learned to separate good martial arts practitioners into two categories: Preservers and Creators. Of course, there are many more categories you could use to slice the population, but let's stick with those two for now.

PRESERVERS

The majority of practitioners - students and teacher alike - are what I call preservers. They study the arts with great passion and try to learn as many techniques and forms as possible. They strive to learn and copy those techniques (and often also their teacher's quotes) as precisely and verbatim as humanly possible.

Most are really good with that and I kind of envy them because my memory usually fails me when I try to learn things by heart.

Preservers are important to keep a style alive the way it was envisioned and practiced by his creator. They are the historians and librarians of martial arts and the styles. However, they often run the risk of thinking that they practice the only correct and legitimate way.

CREATORS

Only a few martial arts practitioners go beyond the limits of what they were shown. They focus on the principles rather than the exact preservation of the movements. They eventually will push beyond what they learned from their teacher and style.

Very often creators will get inspirations from different arts and bring them back into their own art and style, making it richer and more diverse along the way. They will also go down a wrong path much more often than preservers, who stick to the known and tested. Rather than keeping the art precisely as it is, they will help develop it further with time.

Amongst their martial arts peers, creators are not always looked upon too nicely as they don't stick to the official teachings. However, in the end, only creators move the art ahead and keep it alive. If you look back, you will realize that every style and art started with a creator.

One of the trickiest parts of being a creator, however, is to keep the creator mindset alive. All too often creators become preservers once they found their style and from there on insist that everyone follows their rules to the detail.

Uli and I were fortunate to learn from two great creators and martial art

pioneers, Hilmar Fuchs and Roland Habersetzer, right from the beginning. They did spoil us for other teachers though and set a pretty high bar for teachers that we would follow.

While both preservers and creators have their important role in keeping the arts alive, there are two more types that need to be called out. Please try to not be one of them.

COLLECTORS

I met a few over the years. Collectors have a goal to 'master' an art in a certain time. They collect forms, teachings, and teachers with great passion and effort very quickly. They usually make progress very quickly but then drop off completely after a relatively short time.

While there is no harm in doing that, I feel sorry for the time they invest without following through and therefore missing the insights and benefits that can only come over time. They burn fast and hot, but not for a long time.

RANDOMIZERS

Randomizers do not spend enough effort and time to learn an art. They practice but their knowledge remains shallow because their heart and mind are not really at it. Usually, they like to practice, like to sweat or just like the company, but they don't care deeply enough about learning and thus don't invest the time and effort to overcome the pain and frustration that true learning always entails.

Most of them do little harm but some become teachers due to tenure in a style rather than qualification. Learn to spot randomizers quickly and try to stay away from them, especially when they pretend to be teachers (you can often identify them by their dogmatic approach).

"I fear not the man who has practiced 10,000 kicks once, but I fear the man who has practiced one kick 10,000 times."
Bruce Lee

FAMOUS TEACHERS AND THE 'TRUE FORM'

I have to rant a little bit today. I promise to keep it short though. I followed Facebook pages for Tai Chi and martial arts for a few months. I left them all today. I got tired of all the folks out there, who represented the only true, original, traditional, impactful way to do a style, form or exercise.

There is no need to learn the 'true form' from a famous teacher. They are just selling their own personal interpretation like everyone else.

First, find a teacher that teaches principles (!) and spend ample time with him/her to get a solid foundation. It will take several years.

After that, read lots of books, reflect on the ideas and learn to listen to your body, rather than following lots of famous teachers.

Practice, learn and identify the underlying principles. Keep your mind open. Trust your own heart and brain!

Keep the art alive and evolving.

WHY AREN'T MORE PEOPLE PRACTICING TAI CHI?

A student asked a great question in class yesterday: "Tai Chi provides so many benefits for health and memory. It's so important and helpful as we age. Why don't more people do it?"

The short answer is, it's hard work. You can't just attend class, you have to really be in it with your full mind and concentration. Remembering the movements takes effort, and that's just where it begins.

Understanding and applying the principles take your studies and effort to a whole new level. For good reason, the original meaning of Kung Fu (功夫) is 'hard work'. And Tai Chi is, as an internal martial art, part of that family.

Tai Chi introduces powerful changes in your body, mind, and life. But it's not a simple quick fix. It takes time and dedication. As for all things in life that are truly important and truly matter, you have to work for it and you have to be willing to invest the time.

Tai Chi requires more than dropping a pill or showing up for class, going through the motions. You need to learn the individual movements, you need to memorize the form, you need to strengthen and stretch your body, you need to control your breathing, you need to train your mind to be in the moment, while not sticking to a single thing. It's a LOT of stuff that's going on and needs to be mastered.

However, as many studies have shown, the benefits are plentiful, improving strength, flexibility, balance, memory and general health of internal systems. It's tremendously awarding when you start to feel how your balance and your control over your body is improving. It's eye-opening when you experience how applying the principles correctly leads to a whole new level of efficiency and a new perspective of how you experience performing your form. And last not least, Tai Chi has so many layers, that you can practice a lifelong, discovering new insights every day. It never gets boring.

Yes, it's hard work, but it's absolutely worth it! Keep practicing!

LEARN FROM HEART TO HEART

I n martial arts, we teach and learn 'from heart to heart', and 'from skin to skin'.

Many of the deeper principles in martial arts and Tai Chi are hard to explain and hard to understand from just a verbal description. While the intellect might grasp them on a logical level, it's an entirely different thing for the body to be able to execute them in a natural way (what we like to call 'feeling the movement').

We can use books and videos to re-mind our-selves of sequences in a form, or principles that were taught and ex-plained in class, but it's almost impossible to learn new content from them in the beginning years. It's also impossible to spot all the details that are important in a video, and no video or DVD is long enough to allow the narrator to explain them all.

OBSERVE AND ENGAGE

While later on, we extend your knowledge by reading from masters, it is important to learn in class and from a teacher in the beginning. Only with a teacher can we observe all the little details and subconsciously pick up the things, and the energy, that a DVD cannot give us. Only a teacher will be able to spot where we miss important details and correct us before they become hard to change habits.

You learn in martial arts by observing your teacher. Not just through the class but also by observing how she thinks about life and behaves when interacting with others. In the dojo and outside. By observing a real teacher, you will understand how the art taught her to live her life, which will unveil many of the underlying principles and patterns to you. Videos can only get you so far.

OPEN YOUR MIND TO WHAT'S BEHIND IT

In the old days, masters used to have Uchi-deshi (内弟子), inside students, and Soto-deshi (外弟子), outside students.

Soto-deshis were the students that excelled the most in the techniques and the forms. They would win the competitions. They would often be the ones who represented the school and style to the outside world and built up the large organizations. They were also the ones whos understanding often remained shallow and who missed the hidden core of the teachings.

Uchi-deshis lived with their teachers. They weren't usually the best with physical techniques, but they spent a lot of time being with their teachers and observing them. They eventually understood what was under the obvious surface of their art and as a result got taught more of the lesser known underlying ideas and principles.

While we all have busy lives today, try to be more of an Ushi-Deshi than a Soto-deshi. Try to observe and understand the principles and drivers rather than the flashy movements. Observe your teacher as often as you can, not just when she performs the form. Good teachers will show the same principles and respect in outside life as they teach in class. If your teacher doesn't, then run away as quickly as you can.

In martial arts, we learn from observing and practicing. Try to learn from heart to heart and from skin to skin.

> "Don't listen to what I say. Watch what I do."
> Alfons' typical classroom advice

PART II
PRINCIPLES OF
MOVEMENT

Qi follows Yi – Energy follows intent

DON'T BREAK YOUR KNEES!

Our knees are a critical link to make our movements connected and grounded. In martial arts, we start movements from the hip, but actually, if you think about it, the leg muscles are the ones that initiate that movement. And the leg muscles need the knees to transform power into kinetic energy. There is no proper martial arts movement that doesn't start from the knees.

UNDERSTAND YOUR KNEES

The knees are perfectly designed to flex and support your body weight dynamically for that motion. They are not designed for torque or tilt with only limited range for rotation.

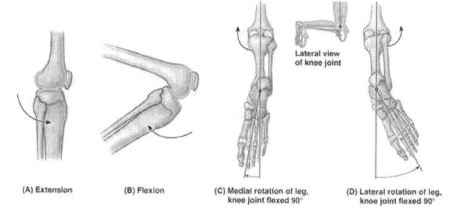

(A) Extension   (B) Flexion   (C) Medial rotation of leg, knee joint flexed 90°   (D) Lateral rotation of leg, knee joint flexed 90°

And that's where the problem begins for many martial arts practitioners and sports enthusiasts. I was one of them. I was doing a lot of athletics and running when I was 16. And my knees hurt almost every day. I was lucky that I met my Karate and Tai Chi teacher Hilmar Fuchs at the age of 20. He taught me how to use my knees properly and equally important, what movements to avoid. Today I'm way older (let's not talk about that right now), I'm still practicing martial arts and running and I have no knees problems at all. I'm pretty sure without Hilmar's intervention I would have had a knee surgery already.

That is precisely why Uli and I put so much emphasis on proper walking and knee utilization in our Tai Chi classes. The classical Tai Chi bow step teaches us many principles about how to use the knee and what to avoid. 'Normal' walking looks different, but the key principles still translate.

PRINCIPLES OF THE BOW STEP

Here is my list of key principles for the bow step that we focus on in our classes:

1. Knees point in the same direction as toes
2. Push the knee no further than over your big toe
3. Keep some flexibility, don't lock your knees
4. Feet are shoulder wide apart
5. Pull weight off a foot before you turn it
6. Hip initiates moves and turns, not the legs, feet or arms
7. Keep your hip on the same level, don't go up and down

The key goal of most of those is to avoid tilt or torque forces on the knee by avoiding to turn against resistance, over-extending or having unnatural angles between the toes and the knee direction. Some of the principles are also meant to most efficiently translate power into kinetic energy, starting a motion with

strong but slow muscles and then engaging weaker but faster muscles. But that's a topic for another blog post.

Pay attention to what you're doing, you want to be able to practice for a lifetime without regular visits to your favorite surgeon.

FOCUS ON YOUR EIGHT POINTS

Focus on your eight points – Always have firm contact to earth with at least 8 points. Be rooted.

ESTABLISH A FIRM ROOTING IN THE GROUND

One of the first lessons we teach beginners is to focus on their 'eight points'. By eight points we mean the eight points of the foot that firmly sit on the ground. Five toes, the balls of your foot, the side of your foot and your heel.

Focusing on your eight points makes you grounded and rooted to the floor. Being mindful of feeling all eight points also prevents you from raising your toes, tilting your foot or lifting your heel when you push forward.

Many times we are connected to earth through 16 points and we're firmly rooted. Some positions only give us 14 points or 9 (you know which ones I'm talking about). As we transition, we temporarily only have eight points. However, it's never less than eight.

All movement is rooted in your feet, then legs, hip and then the upper body. Losing touch and stability in your eight points compromises the strength and stability of your entire movement.

WATCH CHILDREN AND LEARN FROM THEM

Children are perfect with this. As we get older, our mind gets more anxious and we start stiffening all sorts of muscles, leading to raised shoulders, aching lower backs and, yes, curling up toes, tilting feet and lifting heels. Rediscover your inner child and remain firmly connected to earth.

CUT THE STRINGS

C ut the strings – There is only one string left at the Bai Hui point (crown point), everything else drops. Everything above your neck rises, everything below drops.

When we practice Tai Chi we want to relax and lower ourselves down into the center of our body. How do we achieve that?

LIKE A PUPPET ON A STRING

One way is to imagine that we are puppets on a string.

Visualize all the strings that pull you up. The strings on your shoulders, elbows, hands, neck, everywhere... Feel how that pulls and tightens up all the wrong places.

Now imagine how you cut those strings one by one. Cut the strings on your hands and feel how your hands relax and drop. Cut the strings on your elbows and shoulder and feel how you let them relax and allow gravity to pull them down to a natural tensionless state.

Cut all the strings except for one last string that remains: the string from your Bai Hui (百會) point or crown point on the top of your head. This one last string, or golden thread, pulls your head up and keeps your spine and body straight.

LET YOUR HEAD RISE, LET YOUR BODY DROP

The other way of visualizing the same principle is to think about an imaginary horizontal plane that sits at the level of your neck.

Now let everything that is above that plane (your head) rise up, while you imagine everything below that plane becoming heavy and relaxed and dropping down like water drops or like heavyweights falling off your body.

STRAIGHTEN YOUR SPINE, OPEN YOUR JOINTS

Both visualizations help us to relax our muscles by visualizing how everything drops down, straighten our spine by having the golden thread pull up our Bai Hui point and 'open up our joints' by creating tiny spaces between the bones in our joints.

All of that greatly improves our relaxation, agility and energy flow.

OPEN AND CLOSE

O pen and close – Open and close your body like a flower in the
morning and evening. Give out to the universe and focus back
in on your core.

YIN AND YANG

In Tai Chi, we try to constantly flow and change between Yin and Yang.

We borrow some
energy from the
universe, work
with it and give it
back again. We
don't want to keep
it, else it would be-
come stale and
harmful.

We switch from
moment to moment between strong and stable and then flexible and
agile, between expanding out into the universe and then sinking back
deep into our core. In the 'walk of the hero', we switch from proud to
humble to confident in just a few movements.

YOUR MIND FOLLOWS YOUR BODY

It takes a long time to develop that state of mind, to feel the flow between the different opposing states and to finally achieve the merging of
them. A way to practice is by letting our body express those states and
then just watch, listen and learn how that feels.

> "Your body follows your mind. Your mind follows your body."
> Hilmar Fuchs

When practicing your movements, try to make a distinction between opening and closing. Between embracing the universe, giving out all the energy you have and then sinking into your center, retracting and storing the energy for a moment.

IMAGINE TO BE A FLOWER

Turn yourself into a huge energy pump for the universe. Turn your body into a flower that opens its petals in the morning, showing all its beauty to the world and soaking in the sunlight and then goes back and closes for the night to recharge and preserve energy.

Make your movements big and open, contract your back muscles and open your chest and then reverse, bring your movements back to your center, contract your chest muscles and stretch your back.

Practicing open and close will help you to gradually understand the flow between Yin and Yang. It will open your eyes to our role as big energy pumps in the universe (not energy hoarders or energy drains) and it will gently loosen and stretch your torso and limbs.

EMPTY AND FULL

Empty and full – Distinguish between empty and full. Have two containers and pump the water between them.

As we discussed earlier, we put a lot of care in how we move, in order to protect our knees and avoid any tilt or torque on the joints (and with that, possible injuries down the road). We move our weight off a foot before we turn it and back on when it's oriented in the right direction and we're ready to push our Qi Hai (氣海) point forward.

THINK OF YOUR LEGS AS TWO BIG BUCKETS OF WATER

A good way of reminding ourselves of that shifting of weight is by thinking of it as 'shifting between empty and full'. Think of your feet and lower legs as big buckets holding water.

Now when you shift your weight back on your back leg, you envision how that water gets pumped out fo your front leg and into the back leg. Your front leg becomes 'empty'  and your back leg becomes 'full'.

After you turn your hip and with that your foot, you reverse the process, imagining how you pump water through your legs and hips from your back leg into your front leg. Once the back leg is empty you can lift it and make a step.

KEEP THE WATER MOVING

As you make Tai Chi movements, you constantly shift between empty and full and various degrees between. Of course, as you are lifting and moving one leg, the other one is 100% full at that moment. When you are in a bow stance, the front leg is 70% full and the back leg is 30% full. When you are standing on two sides of a line, your front leg will hold 10% of the water while your back leg will hold 90%.

As with everything in Tai Chi you don't hold those static stances, you constantly shift and move, pumping the water, and with that your energy, around. You flow from Yin to Yang and back with all stages in between.

TUCK IN YOUR TAILBONE

Tuck in your tailbone – Lower your hips and tilt them forward. Tuck in your tailbone. Pretend that you are starting to sit down and then stop halfway into the movement.

TUCK IN YOUR TAILBONE

The teacher says "tuck in your tailbone". That's helpful right?

What we mean with that is that you bend your knees a little and slightly tilt your hip forward. You contract the muscles on the front of your lower abdomen and let your lower back gently stretch.

We are often over pronouncing the s-curve in our back (hyperlordosis or hollow back) or in the other extreme hunching over. Contracting the muscles around our lower

hip and 'tucking in our tailbone' helps to avoid both.

When you're asked to tuck in your tailbone, you follow the example from your puppy when he is actually tucking in his tail and visualize that movement. Imagine how you would need to move your hips if you actually wanted (and could) tuck in your tail.

PRETEND TO START SITTING ON A CHAIR

The other way to 'tuck in your tailbone' and achieve the proper posture is to imagine that you're starting to sit down on a high chair.

You bend your knees, lower your hip and tilt it a little bit forward in order to get ready to sit on your behind. Go a little down but stop way before you would actually sit down.

It's as if you are to sit down and then don't.

WORK AGAINST RESISTANCE

One of the big challenges for beginners is to let their center of gravity lead the movements, instead of focusing on arms and hands. Like a strong tree, you want to start from the roots, not from the branches and leaves.

IMAGINE YOU'RE PRACTICING IN A POOL

Visualizing standing in a pool, with water up to your mid-chest, helps to draw a student's mind to the center of her body. If you want to move in a pool, you have to move against the resistance of water. You have to push your waist first, before doing anything fancy with your arms.

Focus on your Qi Hai (氣海) point when pushing and moving forward, focus on your Ming Men (命門) point when pulling and moving back.

LET THE WAVES HELP WITH YOUR MOTION

Once your body has started moving in the pool, you will create motion, momentum and flow in the water. Now visualize how that momentum and flow picks up your arms and your hands and moves them along.

Rather than initiating movements on their own, your arms and hands are propelled by the motion and momentum that's initiated by your center of gravity. They get pulled in by the momentum you create and merely follow the flow of energy.

CHANGE FROM YIN TO YANG

If you keep visualizing the movement in the water, you will also feel how you have to overcome and reverse the momentum in the water as you shift from forward to backward movement.

When you move forward, you create forward motion in the water. Before you can move backward, you have to overcome and reverse that motion. You have to take in the wave and gently turn it backward. And then you reverse the process again as you shift back to moving forward.

We're stirring the water, or the flow of energy, without interruption, shifting between fluid states.

Visualization is a powerful technique to develop a 'feeling' for the moves. Use it!

When we recently practiced 'working against resistance' in class a student afterward told me that it felt "like moving in heavy air". She reflected in her own words, which I had never used in class, exactly the feeling that I wanted to create in students. It was one of the most rewarding things I've ever heard.

"It feels like moving in heavy air."
Student quote after practice

OPEN YOUR LAO GHONG AND YONG QUAN POINTS

O pen your Lao Gong and Yong Quan points – Open and close your hands deliberately. Control and observe the energy flow. Don't trap the energy when you want to push.

We often talk in class about "opening your hands to collect energy" and "cupping the hands to push energy down into our bodies".

What we are really doing is stimulating our Lao Gong (勞宮) points in the middle of the palm of our hands. As we spread out and open up our fingers, we're opening the gate through the Lao Gong points.

THINK OF YOUR ARMS AS A WATER HOSE

Think of it as a water hose. You cup your hands a little, bringing the fingers together to keep the energy in, like pinching a water hose. Then when you let go of the pinch, when you spread out your fingers to open the Lao Gong points, you  open up to let the water (energy) flow.

BECOME A BIG ENERGY PUMP

Now extend that picture and think of your Yong Quan (涌泉) points, in the middle of your feet, as another end of the water hose. Think about pulling water (energy) in through your Lao Gong and Yong Quan points as you inhale, and pushing it out through those four points as you exhale.

Turn yourself into a big energy pump for the universe, connecting Heaven and Earth through yourself (Human).

TRANSMIT YOUR ENERGY

When you push in a movement, think about how you are pushing out energy through your Lao Gong points as you exhale and move your Qi Bai point forward. At the same time push out and connect to the ground through your Yong Quan points.

For example, when you do the double hand pull and push sequence, imagine how you are pulling in water through Lao Gong and Yong Quan when you pull back and inhale. Then reverse and visualize pushing out a sparkling stream of water through those four points as you exhale and push your whole body forward.

"In Tai Chi, we don't keep energy selfishly. We just borrow it for a moment and then give it back to the universe. We connect heaven and earth through ourselves (human)."
Hilmar Fuchs

IT ALL STARTS WITH YOUR FEET

I n martial arts and Tai Chi, we try to learn to make the most effective use of our strength and energy. We learn how to efficiently turn our muscle power into movement and kinetic energy.

BUILD FROM THE GROUND UP

The basic physics law of action and reaction applies to Tai Chi just as well. If we want to exert energy in a given direction, we must also be able to absorb the counter-reaction. So if we want to push forward, we need to be firmly rooted in the ground in order to absorb the push back and not just be thrown backward ourselves.

With that in mind, it all starts from our feet. If we don't have a firm grounding in our stance, everything else falls apart. Be rooted first.

We build up from there, the next link in our chain are the legs and knees, then the hips, our upper body and finally our arms. We need to build up in that sequence or our movement will not unfold its full potential.

Think of a tree, if the roots are weak the tree will die. If the trunk is flimsy it will not be able to withstand the wind. If the branches are too small, the weight of the fruit will have them break down.

SLOW MUSCLES FIRST, FAST MUSCLES WILL CATCH UP

A principle of movement in martial arts is to start with the strong and slow muscles first (our legs and our core muscles) and then engage the weaker but faster muscles (our arms and finally hands). That way we allow all movement to end at the same climactic point - the faster arms and hands will catch up with your legs easily. It won't work the other way around though.

You can think of it like a rocket with its boosters. The huge thrusters engage first to get the rocket off the ground. Then the following smaller and more agile rocket engines will kick in as stage after stage gets engaged. They will further increase the speed of the rocket while making necessary adjustments to the trajectory as needed.

YOUR BREATHING CONTROLS THE MOVEMENT

Let's stay with the image of the rocket for a moment. The sequencing of the different stages is carefully controlled by the mission control center. What's the mission control center in your body? Of course, it's the brain, but there is another way to think about it. In martial arts and Tai Chi, your breath can help  you control and orchestrate the movement.

That's why we pay so much attention to our breath. If we smoothly exhale all the way from the beginning of a movement to its end, it is much easier to make it a smooth movement than if we stop our exhale somewhere along the way or have it disconnected from the movement altogether.

Same if we start our exhale before or after we start the movement or finish before or after we finish the movement. In that case, there is a good chance that we will have stops and breaks in our movement and the different muscles will not coordinate as smoothly as they could. Use your breathing to control your movement.

Tai Chi is meditation in motion. Watch your breathing. Be mindful and deliberate about how your movements build up.

PAY ATTENTION TO YOUR EYES

Mindfulness is an important aspect and benefit of practicing Tai Chi. We practice mindfulness through our focus on the details of the movement and our awareness of our breathing.

What is often overlooked in teaching is what we should do with our eyes or our gaze. It's easy to be so fixated on the moves and techniques that we miss what our students are doing with their eyes.

PERIPHERAL AWARENESS

The general rule in Tai Chi is to not focus your gaze, especially not to stare or get tunnel vision. There are some exceptions from this, for example when we are 'spreading the wings', but those changes in focus are deliberate and consciously controlled.

As we practice, we want to relax our eyes. We avoid staring at any given point, especially we avoid watching ourselves in the mirror all the time. Our gaze should be unfocused, reaching out to the horizon and by that engage and train our peripheral awareness.

As to where that unfocused gaze is oriented, a good rule of thumb is that we should point our head and gaze roughly in the space between your hands. Our eyes are looking into infinity and we should be able to see both hands in our peripheral vision at all times.

BE MINDFUL, BE DELIBERATE

For certain movements, we transition to focusing our eyes. Make this a conscious and deliberate change.

Think of it as your mind discovering something in your peripheral vision that it finds interesting. As it notices that interesting movement, it hones in and focuses. Once examined in detail, you let go and gently go back to an unfocused gaze with peripheral awareness. This trains both mindfulness as well as the essence of martial arts (Zanshin 残心).

Good examples of the above are how we are following our hand when we 'spread the wings' or how we are following our fingers and then let go again in the Qi Gong exercise of 'shooting an arrow'.

Keep your gaze unfocused, in the moment and able to 'see' everything through peripheral awareness. Keep your mind open for unexpected observations. Every now and then something interesting will move into your view and grab your attention. Watch and examine it with a child's curiosity. And then let go again.

FEEL YOUR MOVEMENTS

One last but extremely important thing: learn to 'feel' your movements so you don't have to constantly look in the mirror or at your hands and feet to control what you're doing. Your body needs to learn to give you that feedback, not your eyes.

Don't get into the habit of looking at yourself to control your movements. You can do it every now and then to 'check in', but be very conscious of it and make sure to let go of it again. Looking at our own movements is especially tempting when we have a mirror in the room.

You want to develop a feeling for your movements and you want your body to learn what's right or wrong without having to control with your eyes and your logical brain. Turn off the lights every now and then or simply close your eyes and see what you discover.

"Don't think. Feel."
Bruce Lee

YIN AND YANG – KEEP FLOWING

Yin and Yang – Keep moving, keep shifting. Never stop, never stagnate. Celebrate the black and white instead of perpetual grey.

Everyone talks about Yin and Yang. It's become mainstream folklore to the degree where I was wondering if I should talk about it at all. Then I decided that I needed to because it's too fundamental and important to not call out a few of its core ideas and implications.

The concept of Yin and Yang could fill a whole book on its own (and has done so for many). However here are the aspects I find most important for our Tai Chi practice.

CELEBRATE THE BLACK AND WHITE INSTEAD OF PERPETUAL GREY

On the simplest level, Yin and Yang represent the duality of things in life. Light and darkness, hard and soft, asserting and relenting, open and close, male and female – and we could go on forever. Yin (阴) represents the female and passive, Yang (阳) stands for the male and active.

The first important lesson from Yin and Yang is that we need to actively seek and celebrate the black and white instead of coasting along in perpetual grey.

It is easy to let things drift by, to have one day be just like the other and get dulled in our routines. But if we do so, we miss out on life big time. Rather, we should cherish the ups and downs, the cold and the hot days, the sunshine and the pouring rain for what they are. There is no light without darkness.

In Tai Chi, we focus on developing and feeling those differences. As we progress, we move from executing movements mechanically with the same energy level throughout to developing, feeling and expressing the dualities within. We push and pull, we open and close, we inhale and exhale, we are proud and humble, we are strong and flexible.

As we learn to differentiate and shift between those states of black and white, we experience and enjoy our Tai Chi on a much more intense and rewarding level.

THERE IS YIN IN EVERY YANG – AND VICE VERSA

The second important lesson seems to contradict the first one. It reminds us that there is Yin in every Yang and vice versa.

Even if we are strong, we need to be flexible to some degree. A little less but still. If we are only strong at a particular moment, we become stiff and will break like a frozen twig. If we are only flexible at a given moment, we will be floppy and lack impact, like a soaked sheet of paper.

Now be careful, this does not mean to become grey again. It does not mean to be 80% or 90% strong for example. It means to be 100% strong but to discover the smaller parts within, which still stay 100% flexible at the same time.

This is a difficult concept to think about initially and a hard one to implement. Think about it. Think some more and then try it in your practice. Meditate on the small black circle within the larger white area and try to discover what it might mean for your training and life.

Another way to think about the Yin within the Yang is too look more closely at how we move, how we develop energy and the basic laws of physics (every action creates an equally strong but opposite reaction). When we want to push with one hand, we need to equally focus on the other hand that pulls back. Both are required to develop the proper movement and energy transfer. In Karate, beginners are told that the hand that pulls back in a punch is more important than the fist that thrusts forward. There is a lot of wisdom in that early lesson. Try it out in your form.

LIKE A WAVE – NEVER STOP, NEVER FREEZE

The last important lesson, and here is where I differ with some Tai Chi schools, most importantly the Yang family style itself, is that we need to keep moving and shifting between both states. We need to learn to fluidly go from one to the other without ever stopping.

Tai Chi is not Karate, where we learn to focus all energy in one point and the lock the whole body as we deliver that energy for maximum rigidity and impact. It's also not about delivering the final theater-worthy blow and then stopping and letting the viewer see the dramatic impact as the bad guy crumbles on the floor (Jean-Claude Van Damme does that famously and uselessly in his movies).

In Tai Chi, we want to develop our internal energies and get them flowing first and foremost. We also want to develop a flexible mind, which never gets attached and stuck to a singular thing. In order to do so, we need to train ourselves to keep everything flowing, to remove all the breaks and stops.

Think of your Tai Chi as a wave. It never stops, it never breaks, there is focus, there are climax and anticlimax, but there is not even a single split-second where the moving ever stops. Make your Tai Chi a wave. Go from Yin to Yang and back again. Open and close, inhale and exhale, push and pull - but never stop, never halt. Flow from one into the other fluidly.

Like the water atoms in a wave, everything moves at the same time. Everything reaches the peak at the same time. And in every forward movement, there is a backward movement of some part of your body, like the undercurrent of the wave.

QI FOLLOWS YI

Q i follows Yi – Energy follows intent.

We try to awaken, strengthen and guide our energy through Tai Chi practice. In order to be successful with that, it is not enough to 'go through the motions'. We need to be intentional, deliberate and present when practicing Tai Chi.

QI FOLLOWS YI. ENERGY FOLLOWS INTENT.

Doing the form without intent is a waste of time. Not focusing on the moment misses the main point of what we want to achieve with Tai Chi. Go get a beer and watch a movie instead.

> "Energy follows intent. Qi follows Yi."
> Tai Chi Principle

That is one of the big principles of Tai Chi that all styles agree on. It is hard to explain, but something you develop an awareness of when you work with a teacher (and learn from heart to heart).

Make it a point to always put your mind to what you're doing. Just as in meditation, you will be distracted more than once. You will notice your mind wandering. Gently catch it, bring it back in and focus on what you're doing and why.

While this seems like an esoteric concept, there are actually a few simple exercises that can give you a glimpse into 'Qi follows Yi'. I learned them from an Aikido teacher many years ago when he explained the importance of energy flow to me. Both exercises require a partner.

PICK UP THE KEYS FROM THE FLOOR

Ask your partner to hold your wrist with one or two hands, depending on how the balance of strength is between you. Try to pull your arm out of his grip. Chances are it's hard and in most cases won't work without dirty tricks.

Now imagine there is a set of keys on the floor, right where your fingers point to. Don't think about the grip, just pick up the keys. The first few times you will fail at this because your mind will still be focused on 'breaking the grip'. However, as soon as you relax and put your mind (your intent) into picking up the keys and nothing else, you will find that it is very easy to slip out of the grip. Your Qi followed your Yi.

Many things happen here. For one, you will not signal to your partner that your movement is about to start by activating muscles too early in anticipation of wanting to break free. You will also eliminate any unnecessary movements, like jerking, since all you are focused on is getting down to the keys. Lastly, you will be relaxed and it will be as hard to get a hold of you as it would be to grab a wet wiggly fish.

Put real keys on the floor if you have a hard time to let go mentally. You can also try to pick up the key a few times without having anyone hold you, and then repeat the same movement, ignoring that someone now squeezes your wrist.

WATER FLOWS THROUGH YOUR ARM LIKE A GARDEN HOSE

A similar exercise is to put your hand stretched out on your partner's shoulder, with the palms of your hands facing up. Ask your partner to put both his hands on your elbow joint and try to bend it down. It will be very hard to prevent your arm from being bent, even if you exert all your muscle power.

Now again try to forget your partner and what he is doing. Rather close your eyes and think of your arm as a water hose. Imagine the strong stream of water rushing through your arm and shooting out into infinity. Don't think of your partner, let him do his thing and just imagine the water rushing out your fingertips. Chances are he will not be able to bend your arms and you will not feel that you have to exert a lot of muscle power.

Call it mind tricks if you want. Or placebo effect. Either way, it works!

SPIRAL ENERGY

I n Tai Chi, as well as in martial arts generally, we use spiral movements and energies. Rather than bluntly trying to push through linearly, we use advanced mechanics and drill in like a corkscrew.

WE ALL START WITH LINEAR ENERGY

The most common energy (and thinking) is simple and linear. To get from A to B, we draw a mental line and go straight. To punch, we make a fist and then extend our arm in a straight line. That creates linear kinetic energy that is very much defined and constrained by the strengths in our arms and the velocity in which we can engage our muscles.

LAYER ANOTHER TYPE OF ENERGY ON TOP

In Tai Chi, we don't stop with the simple linear energy. Rather than being constrained by the ability to add more velocity and strength to our arms, we layer a whole different type of energy on top of the movement: spin energy.

As we push out our arm, we also turn it. We add spin to our shoulder, elbow and wrist joints. That does not take away from the linear energy, nor does it extend the length of the movement and thus make it less efficient. It simply layers another type of energy on top of the movement we are already executing. We create a spiral.

SPIRALS INTERTWINED WITH SPIRALS

We don't stop there though. As we execute the movement, we also turn our hip, adding another spin to the movement. We extend our back leg and push our hip forward, creating a linear movement. So there is a second spiral on top (or rather below) the one we discussed before. They are also orthogonal if we want to get into the details of physics, adding further structure and energy dimensions to our movement.

We are creating a system of intertwined and connected layered spirals. We are layering different types of energy on top of each other, thus going way beyond what our arms could ever achieve in isolation.

If you go deeper and look at more details you will discover more spirals throughout. You will discover them in what we are doing with our hands, fingers, core, breathing, feet (as we drill into the earth) and many more.

Tai Chi and martial arts leverage a complex set of efficient spirals in its movements.

SPIRALS ARE EVERYWHERE

Spirals are efficient, which is why we can find them everywhere in mechanics and nature.

If we want to free our hand from a grip we don't just pull, we turn, twist and wiggle. Even little kids learn that pretty quickly.

In a rifle, we have the spiral rifling which adds spin to a bullet to stabilize it and keep it on track (and help it penetrate deeper). Likewise in many sports, we add spin to balls to stabilize them on their trajectory (or make a curveball if we try to be mean).

In mechanics, a screw creates unbelievable linear energy and pull by leveraging spin to create lateral movement.

And lastly, nature gives us endless examples where spirals are used to increase stability and strength of structures and movements. The closest to our heart is probably the very essence of our physical being: the double helix of our DNA.

PART III
AUGMENT YOUR
LEARNING

"Learn and forget. Make the technique a part of
your body before you move on."
Morihei Ueshiba

TAKE NOTES

Our ultimate goal in class is to give students the foundation, structure, and principles to set them on a path where they can advance their own learning and discovery (Shu Ha Ri – How We Learn). In order to do that, a student needs to get to the state where she doesn't need to see and copy the teacher to perform a form or to remind her of a principle.

So there is a lot of stuff that you eventually need to remember as a student.

In my experience, the most effective way to do that is through active learning. Personally, I cannot remember a new form just from doing it two or three times in class once a week. So I take notes after each class. I often only remember one new sequence, but I will write down how I get into that sequence, how the  transitions work and anything that seemed counter-intuitive to me at first (i.e. I won't remember it at home). Over a few weeks, those sequences will add up to the whole form.

That active learning also helps me to process and with that solidify the lesson that I have learned. I make it 'my own' and reinvent the technique or principle in my own mind rather than just letting the teacher entertain me.

Learning requires active engagement with the content. It is hard work (Why Aren't More People Practicing Tai Chi?), but making the content your own is so much more fun and rewarding.

> "Learn and forget. Make the technique a part of your own before you move on."
> Morihei Ueshiba, founder of Aikido

THE FORM IS JUST A CONTAINER

Many students try really hard to remember the form(s). Which is good, it helps us train our memory and it enables students to practice at home and not be dependent on watching the teacher.

However, you should not get frustrated if your progress in memorizing seems too slow to your own standards. Remember that the form is just a container. It matters more what you put into it!

Like with a cup, the container is not the key thing (although some cups are beautiful), it's more important what you put into it. A cup or container can bring back strong feelings and memories, but those memories or feelings always come  from the content or what's associated with the container, rarely from the innate object itself.

In Tai Chi, we'd rather have you strive to understand and feel the principles and energy flows, what you put into the cup than to memorize the form.

Focus on the content, not the container.

THE ANSWER LIES IN THE SMALL DETAILS

We don't need to learn many forms to understand and master the art we're practicing. In fact, trying to learn many different forms often distracts us from understanding the true teachings and underlying principles of our art.

I like to tell students, that we could practice 'stroking the mane of the horse' for the rest of our lives and we would be able to find, practice and perfect all Tai Chi principles within that one movement. In Yang style, it is said that 'grasping the birds tail' is the fundamental movement that represents the essence of the  style. Almost every style has such a movement or essential form, that represents the core of its founder's' ideas (like Kanku Dai for Shotokan founder Gichin Funakoshi and Sanchin for Goju Ryu founder Chojun Miyagi).

THE SMALLEST COMPONENT CONTAINS THE WHOLE

'Stroking the mane of the horse' or 'grasping the bird's tail' seem to be very basic movements, but in fact, all of Tai Chi (and martial arts) is contained in them. As you practice, pay attention to the details and try to find those principles in the simple form.

In science, we learned just fairly recently that all of nature follows a similar rule. The smallest component represents and holds the structure and the principles of the whole. Nature follows the rules of Chaos theory (or System theory in more scientific terms) and is fundamentally of fractal nature. You might know the beautiful and famous pictures of fractals, popularized by Benoit Mandelbrot, which visualize mathematical formulas that describe how our universe is built. If you zoom in, you see the same patterns and rules that you see when you zoom way out. It's the same with Tai Chi, if you zoom

all the way in (e.g. how you move your fingers), you apply and understand the same principles as if you zoom all the way out (e.g. performing the Form of 103).

FOCUS ON THE DETAILS

It also means that you don't have to hold yourself back from practicing on your own just because you don't yet remember the form. If you remember 'stroking the mane of the horse', you have everything you need to practice and understand the principles and details. In fact, you have a higher chance to understand the deeper levels of what you are doing, than when you get stuck on remembering the sequences of the form.

> "The master finds the answers in studying the small details."
> Hilmar Fuchs

So why do we learn multiple forms after all? For the same reason why many systems have graduation levels: to keep the student engaged and interested (in the case of graduation systems also to make more money). If we would practice only one technique for years, most students would get bored and run away. So we switch combinations of techniques and forms to keep everyone mentally engaged.

HOW WE TEACH TODAY

In modern times we are forced to trade avoiding boredom with depth of understanding. In the old days, you would actually have worked on a single form for three to five years, before moving on to the next. For instance, in Karate you would train a form of similar length as the Form of 24 for at least 3 years before your teacher would let you move on to the next one.

Our modern teaching style allows more students to tag along and get benefits, but it requires those who want to really understand their art to go the extra mile and spend the extra effort to go deeper and explore further in their own time. The upside of this approach is that it creates benefits for more people as the arts become more accessible. The downside is that it puts more ownership on students who want to go deeper and understand their art more completely. But then again, maybe that's actually good. No pain, no gain.

The good news is that you get all the tools (principles) in class. Your job is to apply them to your practice. Take individual movements and polish them, using the principles you learned. Follow the principles of 'deliberate practice' (for further reading check out: 'Peak: Secrets From the New Science of Expertise' by Anders Ericsson).

MAKE AS MANY MISTAKES AS POSSIBLE!

So, what should you focus on first in your journey of learning Tai Chi (or any martial art for that matter)? Should you break movements down into sequences and practice those in isolated steps to get all the details right, or gloss over the details to quickly get the feel for the bigger picture? In my mind, it's actually both. Doing one exclusively sets you up for pain further down the road.

BUILD A SOLID FOUNDATION

You do need to spend the time to lay the foundation and take it slow rather than rush-ing on and trying to learn too many different things as quickly as possible. Only a strong foundation allows you to grow in the long-term. Most schools and teach-ers agree on that.

In order to do that you must spend the time to learn the details. Learn a movement and then polish, polish, polish,... Only when you really un-derstand a movement in all its details will you be able to build on it over time. Initially, that will seem to slow your progress down, but over time it's the only way that allows you to grow to more advanced levels of mastery.

Working on the details never ends. Even after decades of practicing you always need to come back to the most fundamental basics. And you will always discover things that you did wrong or got complacent on.

BUT DON'T BECOME A ROBOT!

However, there is also a risk in isolating movements and details too much in the beginning.

I've seen that in my early Karate days when movements were taken apart into stages for beginners and then trained in those isolated stages with the teacher counting the steps through the stages of what should actually be one fluid movement. We all had tremendous difficulties to 'un-learn' those breaks in the movement and make them fluid again.

I've also seen it more recently in Tai Chi classes, where flows were chopped up and breathing wasn't talked about at all for beginner classes. To me that sets you up for a lot of re-learning later on. It makes it harder for your body to 'feel' what Tai Chi (or martial arts) is all about. It also takes away a lot of the fun you get from practicing Tai Chi or martial arts.

IT'S NEVER EITHER / OR

In your practice, you do need both, and in my mind, you should be exposed to both from the beginning.

You need to move slowly and work on the (sometimes boring) details to lay the proper foundation, but you also need to get the chance early on to dip your toes in the water and get exposure to the bigger ideas and principles on movements, body dynamic, breathing and the mind-body connection.

We are not robots after all and we like to understand (at least get a glimpse of) what we're doing and where we're heading.

MAKE AS MANY MISTAKES AS POSSIBLE

In our classes, we try to combine both by spending 90% of the time on the details and basics but then explore 'what's beyond' for 10% of the time. During those 10%, we encourage students to 'make as many mistakes as possible', to free their mind from the details and instead focus on the flow, their breathing and just how the movements 'feel'.

We don't want anyone to be handwavy, but we also want to make sure that even begin-ners start develop-ing a feeling and muscle memory for what the form and flow should feel like and what breathing in sync with the motion might feel like.

We also let them 'run with the form' every now and then, even if they don't know every movement yet. They will make mistakes for sure (like we all still do after all those years of practice), but they will also get a glimpse of where the practice is leading to, which turns out to be ex-tremely motivational for beginners.

It's important to take a conscious break from 'wanting to do it right', from your mind trying to control every detail of a movement, and with that quite frankly often getting in the way. Let your body take over from time to time and good things will happen. That reminds me of an old martial arts story:

A new student asks the master: "How long will it take to learn and master your art?"
To which the master responds: "Ten years."
The student is not satisfied and asks: "What if I study twice as hard as every other student?"
The master replies: "Then it will take fifteen years."
The frustrated student asks: "What if I even double that effort?"
To which the master replies: "It will take twenty years then."

The moral is not to stop practicing regularly and passionately, but rather to let the art develop naturally and not try to force progress, in order to speed up the process.

THE POWER OF METAPHORS

We use a lot of pictures and metaphors when we describe movements or principles in Tai Chi: stroking the mane of the horse, grasping the bird's tail, the white crane spreads its wings, open and close like a flower, grow roots into the ground,... and I could go on forever.

Why do we do this?

Pictures help us to simplify complex combinations of movements, engaging numerous separate muscle groups and our breathing. If we wanted to keep tabs on each of those and every detail to coordinate the muscles properly, we would quickly overload our brain.

That's why learning to drive is so hard in the beginning: we don't' have the picture yet as to what it means to start driving again after you stopped on a steep hill in a stick-shift car. That's why the first weeks are so hard for a new Tai Chi student, as they still try to make sense and coordinate arms and legs.

If we think about metaphors and pictures rather than describing the physics and physiology of a given movement, we take away the task from our conscious brain and give it to our subconscious brain. Our conscious brain is a great single-tasker. It's overloaded quickly with complex problems. Our subconscious brain marvels at complex interwoven systems and tasks. It does that all the time. That's how our organs, breathing and everything vital is kept going. That's what keeps us alive.

If we were to talk to our conscious mind, we would have to say something like this: "Please extend your forearm while also extending your upper arm, twist your elbow and wrist and open the fingers a little bit. Not too much though. Do it all at the same time. Don't forget to breathe! Have we talked about your ankle, knee, and hip yet? Please extend them also at the same time. Don't lift your toes though. By the way, are you all relaxed, joints and all?" (And this is a drastically simplified version.)

That's what beginners in Tai Chi struggle with. As we get more familiar with the basic movements, we don't give our conscious mind these instructions anymore. Rather we tell the conscious mind to imagine 'stroking the mane of a horse' or to 'spread the wings like a crane' and the conscious brain takes that at face value and delegates the complex execution of the details to the subconscious brain, moving on to just enjoy the ride.

Simplify the complex movements for your brain. Keep your conscious mind focused on the big picture and let your subconscious brain deal with the details.

The Chinese are great system thinkers and observers, looking at the big picture and how complex systems work together overall. That's the core of Chinese medicine and that's also how they approached martial arts. In the West, we got a little distracted by Democritus and Descartes who focused us on atomism and reductionism. That has its own benefits and led to huge advancements in science and medicine. It's not the right answer to everything though and for sure it's not the only answer out there (which is how we often treat it these days). Let's learn a little from the Chinese and look at the big picture.

LET YOUR IMAGINATION SOAR

JUST GO AHEAD AND LET YOUR IMAGINATION SOAR

I always ask my Tai Chi participants to let their imagination flow. Feel the wave pushing you back and forth while playing with your balance. Imaging the fresh air flowing into your lungs, pushing a tiny wheel behind your Qi Hai and then pushing the negative energy out of your body again.

It does not really matter what you imagine and the possibilities are endless. Think about playing with an energy sphere between your hands which you can pull and push, or you pull it apart and then it pulls itself back together again.

It can be a round ball made up of swirling energy, you can add some colors, or even sparkles and then throw it in the air to create a rainbow glittering above your head in the sky. Imagine the slime all kids love and play with it if you need a more tactile picture.

PLAY WITH THE ENERGY AND PLAY WITH YOUR VISUALIZATION

Part of this is working on your focus. Kids often start understanding their own bodies by imagining little workers inside of them fighting germs, they make up stories or have imaginary friends. I think it is sad that we lose a lot of that freedom of our imagination along the way of growing up. In Tai Chi, we can focus on this image, feel the energy flow within and use whatever image we want to without even having to tell anyone about it.

One of my favorite movements taught to me by my teacher Hilmar Fuchs is a super simple one. The walk of the warrior. Be proud by lifting up both arms and shifting forward, but also be humble by bending over when shifting backward. Stand back up and be strong and push both arms forward and shift forward. Let everything go and shift back again and be nimble. Repeat to the other corner.

Change it up a bit! Greet the sky and greet the earth, be the human in the middle and the air/wind around us. Or just focus on your breath if you rather feel the air flowing into your lungs.

Tai Chi can carry us into never-ending castles in the sky and at the same time help us to focus on being here in this moment. Feeling and seeing the energy flowing around us.

So go ahead and let your imagination soar.

LET'S GO FLYING

No, I am not talking about levitation. Let your imagination soar and go fly!

Kung Fu, Karate, other martial arts and yes, also Tai Chi Ch'uan have origins showing the spirit of different animals. Think about the Form of 24: Stroke the horse's mane, spread your wings, repulse the monkey, stroke the sparrow's tail, etc. You get the idea.

To go fly, let's choose the crane.

Imagine a great blue heron standing in our wetlands, stalking the fish, patiently waiting and then suddenly picking one out of the water. Or standing there balancing on one leg, maybe sleeping or just being and breathing.

The best example for this is the crane form, Hakutsuru, which is admittedly not Yang style. It originates from Okinawa Karate and before that Kung Fu. Check out the Komatsu-Ha style for it!

But you can find the same feeling in a Yang style form. Open your arms wide, open your fingers like the tips of your wing feathers and play with the opening and closing of your fingers while doing the form. Imagine being a crane, moving through your practice.

Our inner emotions and anxieties often show on our outside. But the opposite is also true. How we present ourselves on the outside can also reflect on our inner well-being. Someone said to me:

"Fake it until you make it!"

One perfect way to feel this is to play with our soaring. Open up your wings and soar in the sky! You could even play with the opposites. Walk through one form rather subdued and then follow it up with a crane flying form. How do you feel?

Let's fly!

HOW WOULD YOUR SPIRIT ANIMAL DO THE FORM?

D o you have a spirit animal? Do you have a favorite animal? Is there an animal always meeting you throughout your life and just showing up whenever you least expect it?

In a lot of spiritual communities animals have a very influential role.

The same can be said for Tai Chi. Tai Chi has roots in Kung Fu and even the names of the moves often refer to animals, for example, 'stroke the mane of the horse', 'stroke the sparrows tail' or 'spread your wings' and more. Feel the movement and try to embrace the animal being mentioned in the move.

Now think about the animal forms of Tai Chi and feel their specific spirit. Do you think about the lumbering bear? The careful and light-footed deer or rather the tiger or the snake?

How do you feel just now? Can you breathe in the specific spirit of this animal and then do the form with this animal in mind?

Each one of the animals has their specific traits and we can show it in our forms. Each animal is connected to different principles of Tai Chi.

CRANE – BREATH

Flying, opening your wings and spreading your fingers. Open your Lao Gong points. Feel the contrast between spreading your fingers and cupping them.

Think about your fingers as the feathers on the wings and feel the wind flowing through them. Hands in clouds lets you soar through the clouds.

Feel the lightness of leaving the earth and feeling the sky. Open up and breathe the air and energy surrounding you.

BEAR – ROOTS

The lumbering heavy bear has you grounded and connects you back to the earth. Feel your balance and your stance on the ground. Be connected through your 16 points.

Feel heavy, but strong. Think about your breath,

going steady and smooth through your moves.

Be aware of your surroundings, but also steady knowing your power.

DEER – MINDFULNESS

Like the bear be aware of your surroundings, but more careful.

Be light on your feet and able to change quickly and lightly into different positions.

Feel the focus, but continue breathing evenly and lightly.

SNAKE – SPIRALS

Slithering over the ground. Twisting your body and your mind and connect it to your movements.

Embody the snake while twisting your joints, opening and closing your body and spine.

Think about spiraling in every move. At the same time be aware of your surroundings. Maybe hiss a little to change your breathing.

TIGER – ENERGY

A force to be reckoned with. Silently and with focus wandering through the jungle.

Embracing its strength and still being aware of its surroundings. There is not a lot they have to be afraid of, but Tigers still are careful.

Feel the strength and the focus in each move. Think about possible martial art applications or the flow of energy providing the support and strength of the movement.

No unnecessary movements there. Everything is focused and simplified.

MONKEY – MOVEMENT

Have fun! Be light on your feet and quick. Transition easily from one move to the other, but still stay focused and light on your feet.

Never forget to play and have fun and don't take everything too serious. Breathe lightly in and out and try to feel like a monkey picking the fruit of the tree.

Switch up the routine and try something new.

YOUR SPIRIT ANIMAL

Now come back to your spirit animal, if you have one, and try to think about their specific and unique traits and try to infuse them into your movements.

I like to mix up the forms every now and then and show the specific trait of the animal. Don't be afraid to be playful like the monkey or twist and spiral like a snake. Maybe lumber like the bear or show the Tigers power. And last but not least be the crane, being rooted on the ground but also opening up to breath and spreading your wings!

And sometimes be like the little mouse - my spirit animal - and be quick and curious and careful at the same time. Switch between deep breath and light breath, move and twist and just be playful.

REMEMBER THE FEELING, NOT THE EXPLANATION

In our last class, we focused on pushing from the Qi Hai (氣海) and Ming Men (命門) points. It was an exercise to draw students' attention to their lower bodies and to initiating all movement from there, instead of overthinking the arms.

After class, when I asked everyone how the exercise worked for them, one of my students said: "that felt different". I wanted to hug her at that moment. Instead, I went on explaining that this is exactly what we want to achieve.

Very often we get too busy trying to remember and follow the explanations. We need to memorize all the details in our conscious mind and then try to recreate the mechanics and choreography every single time. It's a daunting task and extremely hard to do for our logical brain.

REMEMBER THE FEELING

There's actually another part of our brain that's much better suited for such tasks: the subconscious brain.

Instead of trying to memorize the choreography of complex movements, rather remember how it 'felt'. Let you body experiment with the movements and when it feels right (or different), remember that **feeling**. In subsequent repetitions, try to rediscover that feeling, not the prescribed details of the movement.

Move the complexity to coordinate your limbs to the subconscious brain and the body. That's what both have been perfected for through thousands of years. The logical brain is a much newer invention and should rather focus on awareness (Zanshin, 残心) and mindfulness to what we're doing. Let your mind observe and follow what your body and subconscious brain have learned to do instead of trying to micromanage them.

Focus on the feeling, not the explanation! Try to rediscover the feeling instead of trying to execute against a complex set of mechanical directions.

Ever heard of the term 'muscle memory'? ;-)

LEARN AND FORGET

Morihei Ueshiba, the founder of Aikido, once said "Learn and forget. Make the technique a part of your body before you move on."

It's one of the key principles I followed in my studies and well as in my life. Partly because I have a poor memory for details, partly because it makes a lot of sense.

> "Learn and forget. Make the technique a part of your body before you move on."
> Morihei Ueshiba

WHY WE NEED TO FORGET

Learn and forget. How does that make sense and what do we mean by that?

The idea is not, to not pay attention at all or to be a lazy student. Rather the opposite. The idea is to practice a technique, a movement or a form until you can repeat it correctly. By that time you understand the representation and interpretation that was shown to you by your teacher.

At that point, you are either stuck or you can move on to the next level. In order to move on, you need to free yourself from the representation and interpretation you were shown and you have to recognize and understand the essence of what you're doing. You then have to rediscover its representation within your own framework of experiences, philosophies and physical abilities.

You 'forget' what you were taught and you rediscover the underlying essence within your own framework. You make the technique 'yours'.

REPEAT A HUNDRED TIMES TO MAKE IT STICK

Before we can forget and rediscover in our own framework, we first have to sufficiently understand (and remember) what we're doing, so that we have a basis to understand the core and evolve our understanding from there.

That is where we have to repeat a hundred times to make it stick. We need to take notes after class, to reflect on principles and new learnings and make them sit. We need to embrace active learning, asking questions and repeating what we learned within 48 hours to commit it to long-term memory. Ideally, we teach what we learned to another person to test and solidify our understanding.

Learn and forget – rediscover the teachings for yourself, with your own abilities and constraints.

HAVE FUN AND ENJOY THE RIDE!

DON'T TAKE IT (AND YOURSELF) TOO SERIOUS

We talked a lot about principles and how we learn in Tai Chi, martial arts and beyond. Now here's my most important lesson: "Whatever you do, have fun and enjoy what you're doing!" Don't take yourself and the art that you're practicing too serious.

This is not your work. You choose to come every single time you go to class or practice on your own. You invest a lot of time and energy. You might as well enjoy it and have fun.

Take it easy, there is no one who judges you - unless you let them. This is not your work. There is no goal that you need to achieve, there is no deadline. Relax, let go, open your mind to what presents itself and enjoy the ride!

Laugh at yourself as often as you can. And if you have a teacher who is deadly serious and cannot laugh about (or admit) his own mistakes - run as fast as you can.

"This is not your work. You might as well smile and enjoy what you're doing!"
Alfons' regular reminder in class

SEND A SILENT SMILE TO YOURSELF

When you practice Tai Chi, don't just go through the motions of the form. Use Tai Chi to generate and direct positive energy to yourself and the people training with you.

Smile and then send that smile to yourself and to the different parts of your body that you are working with. Send a smile to your lungs as you inhale and be mindful of the air streaming into your lungs. Send a smile to your heart and your inner organs. Send a smile to your skin as you brush over it.

Be mindful of what you do and then engage your mind for healing.

Always be gentle and nice to yourself. In Tai Chi, we don't forcefully push our limits. We discover our boundaries and then gently push into them. Over time they will widen and become limitless. We don't need to break our body on the way.

Gently stretch. Ask your mind and your awareness to follow what your body is doing. Send a smile to your heart, your lungs and your inner organs and thank them for the work they are doing for you!

"Send a silent smile to your heart!"
Marlene Fuchs

PART IV
TAI CHI FOR HEALTH

"The teacher only opens the door. The students
walk through it on their own."
Hilmar Fuchs

THE THREE LEGS OF A STOOL

Why do we learn and practice Tai Chi? Everyone has a different motivation, but essentially Tai Chi spans three big areas: physical health, mental well-being, and martial arts.

We will focus on the benefits for health and well-being in the following chapters. The martial arts aspect would require its own book or might be covered in a future edition of this one.

PHYSICAL HEALTH

Chinese people have known and enjoyed the health benefits of Tai Chi for centuries. Recently western medicine picked up on it as well and by now there are countless studies that show the long-term health benefits of Tai Chi.

While Tai Chi cannot replace medical treatment for illnesses, it can certainly help with recovery or ease the pains of various diseases and ailments. Tai Chi also helps us to age more gracefully and healthy.

Tai Chi is a holistic and gentle exercise system. Where western medicine focused on isolated sub-systems for a long time, eastern health practitioners always looked at the whole human being holistically. Tai Chi reflects that approach.

By practicing Tai Chi, we slowly extend the capabilities of our bodies and over time build up resilience, strength, and flexibility.

MENTAL WELL-BEING

Tai Chi is often referred to as 'meditation in motion'. We pay close attention to our movements, our gaze, and our breathing. We are aware of every little detail as well as how they connect together to the bigger whole.

That focus and awareness help us calm our minds and tame the random thoughts that usually chase us through the day. We take a break from the hectic of the day and reconnect with our inner selves.

With that, Tai Chi is an excellent counterbalance to stress and helps us to step back and take a broader perspective. Our minds calm down and many things that had upset us before class appear in a different light afterward and seem less daunting than they did before.

We also learn that everything come in waves. Everything is Yin and Yang. The same is true in life. There is stress and there is relaxation (if we are willing to allow us to find it), there is frustration and there is joy.

Tai Chi is a great metaphor for the flooding and ebbing of life and by examining and understanding Tai Chi we can develop a greater understanding of life itself.

MARTIAL ARTS

Tai Chi originated from a martial art. Today different schools put different emphasis on Tai Chi as a martial art versus Tai Chi for health. In our school, we focus on the health aspect, but we also personally have our roots in the martial arts and have always been fond of exploring possible applications. We just don't believe that the martial aspect is the most valuable thing we can get out of Tai Chi practice.

With that I mean, that as you progress you should try to understand possible applications to more deeply understand the form and Tai Chi itself. However, I don't think that the ultimate goal is to be unbeatable in push-hands. If pure self-defense is your goal, go and buy some pepper spray or a gun, it's a way easier and faster path.

Unlike what some folks on the Internet will tell you, Tai Chi is not a secret martial art that gives you magic powers to control others without even touching them. You will not be unbeatable since real combat is way different from what you experience in the training hall, with friends pretending to attack you. Real street thugs are vicious and unless you train for that scenario specifically, you will not be prepared. It's more dangerous to fool yourself into a wrong sense of control than to be aware of your gaps and conscious of your surroundings.

However, Tai Chi has originated from, and still is, an internal martial art, and if you study it for a LONG time, the movements will become natural and turn into reflexes. You will be more aware of your surroundings and might be able to use some reflexive moves for initial self-defense. After creating that short opening, you run and dial 911!

Likewise, if you are practicing another external martial art, Tai Chi will for sure improve your grasp of that art and make it more effective. The slow movements and principled approach of Tai Chi will allow you to grasp the underlying principles of body mechanics as well as martial applications. Tai Chi will greatly enhance your understanding of your original art like it did for our own Karate understanding. Eventually, it will all blend together into the system that works for your specific body and background.

Whatever reason brings you to Tai Chi, make sure you also experience the other aspects. Don't become a one-legged stool, they are rather useless.

"Learn Tai Chi Ch'uan, and you will become agile like a child, strong like a wood-cutter and calm like a wise man."
Chinese proverb

STRETCH GENTLY

C ontrary to many other sports, we are trying to not 'try too hard' in Tai Chi. That sounds funny, doesn't it?

What I mean by that is that we give ourselves time to develop balance, flexibility, and strength. We don't go to the point where we think we achieved something because our body hurts.

I'm not saying there is no value in cardio and strength training that pushes and expands the limits of our body. What I'm saying is that this is not how we do Tai Chi or what we want to achieve with Tai Chi. Having a different approach to how we exercise is also the main reason why we can practice Tai Chi and gain health benefits from it, no matter our age or abilities.

TAP GENTLY AGAINST YOUR BOUNDARIES

In Tai Chi, we don't push too hard. Rather we discover our boundaries and gently and slowly push against them. We gently stretch and make sure we don't strain any muscles by trying too hard. We slowly lower our stance over time,  making sure that we are not harming our joints by trying to go too deep too quickly before our muscles had a chance to develop properly. We are gentle and soft instead of hard and inflexible.

Every time I show in class what pushing too hard means, even for basic exercises like connecting heaven and earth, I come home with some strained muscles in my back. Someday I will learn to just not show wrong execution anymore...

Think of the flower fists. We're not making a board-breaking fist, but rather imagine that we hold a precious rose in our hand and we certainly don't want to squish it.

WE ARE IN IT FOR THE LONG RUN

In Tai Chi, we gently push our limits. We develop new abilities slowly but consistently, without interruptions by strained muscles or unwanted knee surgery. We're in for the long run and for a lifelong practice.

The next time you feel frustrated because you cannot stretch as much as the person next to you, you cannot lower your center as easily as your teacher, or your balance is wobblier that everyone else's - let go! Practice Tai Chi within your own limits and abilities. No one else matters. Don't push it too hard but give yourself the time your body needs to develop.

The constant flow of water breaks the rock over time.

LOOSEN YOUR JOINTS

The Yang style is expansive. We try to reach out into the universe, and then come back to our core (open and close).

CREATE SPACE BETWEEN YOUR JOINTS

One of the things we try to do is to create a little space between our joints. Imagine that you are opening up, let's say when creating a big circle with your arms. Now imagine that you pull your bones apart a tiny bit further so that you create a little space between your joints.

As you come back, you compress that space again. Think about your cartilage tissue and your discs like sponges. You compress them, and then you re-lease them again.

We do this with all our joints as well as with our spine as we stretch out and then come back again. That movement squeezes and extends our discs and cartilage. It twists and compresses. We create movement and activate energy and drive out staleness. By squeezing and twisting we pump fluids through discs and cartilages and nurture them.

SQUEEZE LIKE A SPONGE

It really is like a sponge. If you want to clean it, you need to squeeze and release it and then rinse and repeat.

Like for a clogged pipe, we remove blockages by twisting, pressing, pulling and shaking. We release blockages and get our energy flow unstuck.

The same effect works on our inner organs as we stretch, twist and bend our body. Tai Chi movements provide and gentle massage and vitalization for our inner organs, discs, and cartilages.

STRENGTHEN YOUR CORE

The Chinese say that if you practice Tai Chi correctly and regularly, you will gain the pliability of a child, the health of a lumberjack and the peace of mind of a sage.

In Tai Chi, we are not pushing weights and we are not focusing on pumping up our biceps or shoulders. However, we constantly move our body. We shift and twist, we stretch and bend.

In order to do so, we leverage proper posture to support our body without the need for excessive muscle support. However, we constantly engage our core muscles to stabilize and center ourselves.

Tai Chi is a great exercise to learn the proper body mechanics and postures that are self-supported and keep us pain-free without tiring. It's also a gentle, yet effective way to train the core muscles that support our body.

Our arms are just extensions in Tai Chi forms. Power and energy are created from our feet, our legs, up through our core and only as the last step through our arms. If you want to be really strong and unmovable, you need a strong foundation and core.

Gain the pliability of a child, the health of a lumber-jack and the peace of mind of a sage through the practice of Tai Chi.

IMPROVE YOUR BALANCE

DON'T LOSE YOUR BALANCE!

One of the big long-term benefits of Tai Chi is that it helps us improve our balance. Especially as we get older, it becomes harder and harder to maintain good balance and if we don't deliberately focus on improving it, we will lose it. That leads to a higher rate of falls which, together with lower bone density, leads to more fractures and second-ary health risks.

Improving balance in Tai Chi is not about standing on one leg and kick-ing - although we occasionally do that as well. Much more than that, it

is about building a stable base on the ground from which all other move-ments originate, whether we are practicing a form or just going about our daily lives.

PUSH INTO THE GROUND

To improve the balance of our stance, we start by getting rooted. Rather than struggling to balance the upper parts or our body, we try to push our feet into the ground. We remember the eight points and we try to sink them into the ground as deeply as we can and get 'rooted'.

An extreme example of this is when we try to balance on one leg. Try focusing on your upper body and balancing that, and you will find it pretty hard. Then try to forget about your upper body and instead focus solely on pushing your standing leg down as much as you can (while lowering your hips) and you will find balancing a lot easier.

If you want to go up, you need to put your focus on pushing down!

LIKE A PYRAMID

Once you have laid the foundation through rooting, the second important piece is to build a strong base to stand on.

Make sure that your knees are in a straight line with your toes at any time. You can visually check this as you practice. Your knees need to be pointing straight to your toes or just be covering them visually.

Now make also sure, that you have a little outward tension on your knees. Don't let them drop inside. Feel like you have little rubber bands that pull your knees outward. You want to feel like a pyramid that has a pointy top and then consistently grows outward and larger towards the bottom.

Think of tent lines. The first step in pitching a tent is to firmly lock it to the ground with the base tent nails. That still doesn't provide maximum stability though. In the second step, you now need to take the lines on the tent skin and pull them outwards where you fix them in the ground to maintain proper tension.

Be a tent that has proper tension. Don't be a soggy tent without stabilizing lines that will fall apart at the first blow of wind or leak as the raindrops fall.

Keeping your knees in line with your toes is essential for stability, but it is also critical to keep your knees healthy and avoid injury. Remember: avoid torque or tilt on your knees!

"Stability creates confidence. Confidence creates calmness."
Alfons

TRAIN YOUR BRAIN

Train your brain and keep it sharp!

Your brain is just like your muscles. Use it or lose it. You train it and you will keep up its performance, or you get lazy and it will degenerate.

It's proven that both mental exercises but also physical exercises help us keep our intellectual capacities. Tai Chi gives us both stimuli.

We often say that we learn the forms to not get bored. That's only half of the truth though. Learning the form also forces us to stay alert, to listen and watch with focus, and memorize complex sequences.

Tai Chi stimulates us through physical exercise. It teaches us to focus on one thing and one thing only and get the most mileage out of our mental capabilities. It also keeps our brain engaged by keeping up and memorizing all the things that our teacher throws at us.

Practice Tai Chi and stay sharp!

LEARN TO BE IN THE MOMENT

Tai Chi is often called 'meditation in motion'. Like meditation it keeps our mind focused in the here and now. Achieving that focus in Tai Chi actually comes easier to me than in meditation because I have more things to focus on (the movements) and my mind is less easily distracted by other thoughts. I simply don't have the bandwidth to think about other things.

In Tai Chi, we focus on our breathing, the specific movement, the sequencing in the form and the underlying principles. Most days that is enough to chase away other random thoughts, like what we still need to do at home, the person on the  street that really bothered us, or any number of other distracting things.

Being focused in the moment and on what we are doing right now calms us down. It restores our mental balance.

Through practice, we learn to enjoy the NOW. To relax, to keep your sanity and not to fret about the past or obsess about the future.

Tai Chi is no magic cure, but it helps us practice that focus and calmness, and to bring it over to our day-to-day life one step at a time.

YOUR POSTURE DEFINES YOUR MINDSET

Tai Chi can help you shape your posture and with that also re-define your mindset.

When we try to be centered, we are not only influencing the physical structure of our body but also our mindset. When we try to be relaxed, we impact our body, but also our mind. When we try to exert energy, we not only push with our muscles, but we also develop our focus and intent.

YOUR MIND REFLECTS ON YOUR POSTURE, YOUR POSTURE REFLECTS ON YOUR MIND

Another one of the early lessons our teacher Hilmar Fuchs taught us is, how the communication between body and mind is bi-directional.

If our mind is sluggish, our techniques are weak. If we feel depressed or just tired, we have a ten-dency to hunch down instead of hav-ing the golden thread pull up our crown point. If we feel strong and confident, we will make big-

ger movements, embracing the universe and conquering the world.

But it also goes the other way. If we start Tai Chi tired, but focus on finding our center of gravity, focus on opening and on wide movements, we will feel how our energy and confidence increases. If we are all stirred up and restless when we start practice but focus on our breathing and the slow but fluid movements, we will observe how our mind calms down and finds its own center.

How we feel influences how we hold and move our body. But more importantly, it also goes the other way: by controlling our postures and movements, we can control and shape our mental state and how we feel. This is a powerful tool (and much better than any drugs)!

"Your mind reflects on your body. Your body reflects on your mind."
Hilmar Fuchs

While this connection has been long known in martial arts and eastern health systems, it has recently been shown by western science as well. If you want to do some further reading on the scientific background for this, I would recommend to check out Amy Cuddy's book 'Presence: Bringing Your Boldest Self to Your Biggest Challenges'.

WALK OF THE HERO

One of the best exercises to feel this direct connection between body and mind is the 'Walk of the hero'.

The point of this exercise is to shift from proud and bold to small and humble and then to centered and calm. From reaching out, externally focused, Yang-heavy to coming back to your core, inside oriented, Yin-heavy, to then finding the perfect balance between the two.

Observe your mind and feeling before you do this exercise. Then do it for a few minutes and see if anything has changed. You will be surprised!

IMPROVE YOUR SENSITIVITY AND AWARENESS

Tai Chi and martial arts help us to improve our sensitivity and awareness. They help us to achieve a deeper level of mindfulness throughout our lives.

SENSITIVITY

While we initially mostly struggle to follow our teacher's direction, we will notice over time that Tai Chi creates its own sensations as we go through our practice. We learn to listen to our body and we notice the small changes and feedbacks that we are getting. Tai Chi becomes more than just 'going through the motions'.

That change creates a deeper awareness of our movements, our body, and our mental and emotional state. We become more observant, aware and reflective. Tai Chi constantly teaches us to observe ourselves very closely in order to monitor whether we are doing the moves properly.

Observing is the first step to changing. Tai Chi prepares us to build up an effective feedback loop to better control our own reactions to the things that life throws at us.

We are more aware, live more in the moment and with that, we learn to enjoy life more.

AWARENESS

The other kind of awareness that we gradually build up as we study Tai Chi is situational awareness.

All too often, we go through our days without noticing what is happening around us. Remember those funny videos where people bump into objects because they are fully immersed in their smart phones?

Tai Chi, as any worthy martial art, teaches us to have both attention to the detail when needed, as well as situational awareness throughout. In Japanese martial arts that situational awareness is called Zanshin (残心) and it is a core building block for all traditional Japanese martial arts. The best technique doesn't do nique doesn't do

you any good if you don't see the bad guy coming.

We train our gaze in Tai Chi. Most of the time we have an unfocused peripheral view. When appropriate, we focus in on an important detail and then we let go again. If you do that consciously, it becomes a natural habit throughout your days.

However, you don't only need this to become a legendary warrior. Being aware of your surroundings lets you more deeply appreciate the beautiful world we're living in. It will make you more aware and thus safer, but it will also make you more tuned in to your life and thus happier. It might even take your relationships to a whole new level if you pay attention to the other person!

"Live in the here and now!"
Zen principle

GO OUTSIDE

Whenever you can, try to go outside for your Tai Chi practice.

CONNECT TO NATURE

Tai Chi is a great way to connect with your inner core as well as with the universe around you. Practicing outside is a shortcut to the latter one, breaking down the walls that normally separate us from nature.

Connect with nature and heal. Inhale the fresh air, focus on the smell of flowers in spring and the sweet flavors of fruit in fall (we always smell blackberries around here). Take in the salty sea air or the fresh mountain breeze. Experience dry

deserts or cooling forests. Listen to bird songs and nature sounds.

"Be in the moment and be connected to nature!"

MAKE IT REAL

The other benefit of going outside for your practice is that it adds a whole new layer of sensations and complexity to your practice.

While our inside training rooms are perfectly leveled, with smooth floors and air condition, nature is much less predictable. The ground is rough with sudden holes, the sun might shine in your eyes and blind you, the wind might tickle you and the bugs might annoy you.

That means lots of stimuli and lots of distractions. Learn to deal and eventually to work with it. Life is messy, learn to manage your arts within that messiness. If your art only works in controlled environments, it actually doesn't work at all.

Work with and embrace distractions. Learn to do perfect your Tai Chi in an imperfect setting.

YOU ARE NEVER TOO OLD

There is no right or wrong way

I might not be mainstream with this, but one of the things I love about Tai Chi is the possibility to adjust it to your own body, to your own abilities and restrictions.

And yes, you can and should adjust Tai Chi as needed. Even feel encouraged to do so!

There are enough studies nowadays, showing that Tai Chi helps with Balance, Breathing, Osteoporosis, Fibromyalgia and all kinds of other maladies, but how can it affect all those different areas of your life and body, when we all do exactly the same? We are all different with our bodies and we all start at a different  level of ability with our Tai Chi journey. So just feel free to adjust it in any way necessary.

Yes, of course, we look at all those older Chinese people in the park practicing their Tai Chi and admire their flexibility, fluidity, and low stance, but is that really necessary?

I do not think so.

To reap the benefits of Tai Chi, we have to start somewhere and cannot and should not try to do what others do. We have to use the principles we are learning and just move! It does not matter if the form looks perfect or not, it is important to move and breath and focus. It is not important that your hand is in that specific angle, or your foot has to be 45 degrees and your stance has to be this low.

We all have our specific abilities and restrictions and we have to work with those. So feel your own body, follow your gut feeling. If something does not work for you, don't do it. Change it in a way, which won't hurt and start working on it. The journey always starts with the first step. So if at first, you are not able to lift your arms, start with minimal movement. If your body prohibits bending down, just start with moving your spine. Round it, tug in your tailbone, round your shoulders. In the end, we want to work on our flexibility, slowly improving it, but not forcing it.

If balance is an issue, sit down. Slowly start with short periods of standing up and holding on to the chair. You might not be able to practice a form, but use the principles to move.

Adjust what you're doing to your abilities. Think about principles, not perfectionism. Start with those and over time, your body will follow.

PART V REFLECTIONS ON MARTIAL ARTS AND LIFE

Black belts are just white belts that never stopped trying.

SLOW IS SMOOTH, SMOOTH IS FAST

Tai Chi is an ancient martial art and all movements are rooted in the original fighting application. Many schools still teach Tai Chi as a fighting system, using energy and strong rooting to imbalance an opponent, much like the Japanese Aikido.

OUR MAIN PURPOSE IN TAI CHI IS HEALTH IMPROVEMENT

Personally, I put more focus on the health aspects of Tai Chi. I studied Karate for a long time and am pretty sure I would go back to those techniques if I ever needed to defend myself. I studied Tai Chi over the same duration so it's not about new versus old habits. Plus if you want to be able to defend yourself effectively with a short learning ramp you should buy pepper spray anyways.

Most people who come to our classes follow the same goals (I know, it's selection bias). They want to learn Tai Chi for health, for balance, as an antidote for stressful jobs and to improve their mindfulness. They do know the movements originate in martial arts and we often show potential applications to more fully explain the movement, but it's not why they are practicing Tai Chi.

However, occasionally one wonders if Tai Chi would actually create the right reflexes that are needed to defend oneself if ever needed. Especially if a student focuses on the form, precision in movement, flow, and the typical slow, deliberate execution, but not on exercises with a partner like push hands. Furthermore, we practice Yang style, so we don't have the explosive techniques in-between that the Chen style teaches.

MUSCLE MEMORY - POLISH, POLISH, POLISH

I think Tai Chi, even when practicing the form, builds up those reflexes over time. You won't become a hand-to-hand combat strategist or skilled offensive attacker, but your muscles will learn self-defense movements and those will turn into  muscle memory and eventually reflexes.

Don't focus on the application, your body will react through reflexes anyway. Focus on the proper execution of a movement and the other pieces will fall into place.

"Wax on, wax off."
Mr. Miyagi in Karate Kid

Of course, it will take years but then again, that's not why we are doing Tai Chi, to begin with and we hope to never use those skills anyway. If you are looking for a quick solution, buy pepper spray.

SLOW IS SMOOTH, SMOOTH IS FAST

In my personal opinion, I also don't think one must try to execute movements fast. One should try to execute them correctly, with minimal waste through unnecessary movements, keeping all muscles relaxed and as smoothly as possible, flowing from one movement into the other without interruption.

As you build up energy flow and smooth out blockers, you will build up speed and force. Water breaks the rock. Remember the old saying:

"Slow is smooth, smooth is fast."
Wyatt Earp

If your movement is fluid, it will be fast when it needs to be.

NO RANKS, NO TITLES

I love the Gore company tagline "No ranks, no titles"!

In the Tai Chi we practice and teach, we don't care about ranks and titles. We do care about knowledge and respect for each other a lot, but not about artificial ways to express those. If you need a rank to get respect and authority, you have other more pressing issues to address.

So why do many systems have ranks? There's a simple answer: to make money. You pay fees for examinations, for memberships, for special training. You pay your way into the hierarchy. In the old days, even in systems that had a ranking, your teacher would someday just come to you and say: "Congratulations, you reached the next level of understanding".

If you are looking for certificates and ways to slowly level yourself about others, you won't be happy in our classes. If you seek understanding and encouragement, you might have found your place.

Don't get me wrong. I've been there. I went through 9 student ranks in Karate (Kyu 級 grades) and 3 black belt ranks (Senpai 先輩 grades) through the formal system, before I understood that it doesn't matter. I stopped chasing ranks after that. My 4th black belt was given to me by my teacher after a regular training session, to my big surprise (I'm still surprised, to be honest).

I never called my teacher "sensei" (先生) and he never wanted that, but it was always clear to me that he is my teacher and role model. He is an 8th-degree black belt, so he would have all reason to be called "sensei". It just doesn't make any difference, other than creating an unnatural gap between the two of us.

Why would you need a ranking system? Either you know what you're doing or you don't. Either you have something to teach or you don't.

Ranks are a way for organizations, not great teachers, to make money and make students stick around because it takes time to pass the mandatory wait times as you buy your way through the ranks.

Rather than chasing a rank, spend time with your teacher, listen to what he says and learn. That's all that is needed. Focus on the art, not on the distractions.

If your teacher insists that you call him "Master", "Sensei" or "Sifu" (師傅) and wants to push you through the grades, then very politely thank him. Then go and find a real teacher.

HOW MANY DIFFERENT ARTS SHOULD YOU EXPLORE?

How many different (martial) arts should you explore? Pick one and practice it over your lifetime to become the expert of experts? Switch frequently and try as many as you can to have the broadest possible perspective? I think the answer lies somewhere in the middle.

If you only ever study one art, chances are you will not fully understand it. If you get distracted by trying to do too many, then most likely you will not get anywhere with either one.

AVOID TUNNEL VISION

While I strongly believe that you need to spend a lot of time on one art to really under- stand it, and maybe eventually even master it to some degree, it also limits your perspective to a problem and its solution to only one single angle.

I often noticed that I would understand things on a deeper level when they were presented to me from different angles. Sometimes the Karate explanation made more sense to me, sometimes it was the Tai Chi approach and sometimes I would finally understand a difficult principle while trying to practice an Aikido move or Jodo strike.

DON'T MISS THE TREE FOR THE FOREST

On the flip side, you need deep and enduring exposure to a certain framework of thinking or philosophy, to understand it on a natural level, to feel it. To "make it yours" (Morihei Ueshiba).

So if you try to learn too many different things at the same time, it will distract you more than it will help. It's hard to combine teachings from external arts like Karate with internal systems like Tai Chi if you didn't get to the level of seeing the principles yet. It will all just seem like a big mess of disconnected contradictions.

KNOW YOUR CORE AND EXPAND FROM THERE

Start by picking one martial art. Practice it. Practice some more. Keep practicing until you reach a level where the underlying principles start revealing themselves and until you don't have to 'think' about the movements anymore.

Then go and add small doses of other styles and arts to it. Observe what that teaches you. See what new angles and perspectives open up for problems that you already worked on (and maybe struggled with). Be open to understanding moves that you have already practiced from a new and different angle. Don't rip and replace, rather add to your knowledge.

You might shift your primary art over time as your interests change, but always have a primary art that you go deep on and see others as supplements.

If you experiment with other arts, I would recommend seeking significantly different perspectives. If you do Shotokan Karate, don't do Wado Ryu. It will teach you a master's preferences, but only a few new insights. Add something different like Aikido or Tai Chi. If your focus is an external martial art (like Karate, Kung-fu, Tae Kwon Do, etc) then add an internal art (like Aikido, Tai Chi, etc) and vice versa.

Dip your toes into something new. Try it out long enough to get a good sense of the ideas and principles underneath, but know your home base. Know your core and expand from there.

LIKE CLIMBING A MOUNTAIN

WHAT IS THE DIFFERENCE BETWEEN STYLES?

We often get asked about the differences between different arts like Qi Gong and Tai Chi, different styles like Yang and Chen or even between internal (e.g. Tai Chi) and external (e.g. Karate) martial arts.

There is a lot of commonality between all of them. They all agree on similar fundamental principles since they all aim to do the same thing: maximize the effectiveness with which we use our body. Since we all fundamentally have the same physiology and live within the same laws of physics, the principles must have a lot of overlap.

There are also some obvious differences in terms of the focus areas and priorities we set in the different arts. Some arts put a lot of emphasis on speed and force, like Karate, Kung Fu or Boxing. Others try to use an opponent's energy and turn it against him, like Aikido or Tai Chi. Some focus completely on the inner awareness and energy flows like Qi Gong, Yoga or meditation.

None of them is better than the other and all of them complement each other. We try to increase and improve energy and its flow in our classes, so we add energy-focused Qi Gong exercises in the beginning before we focus more on the flow and movement of the Tai Chi forms.

LIKE CLIMBING A MOUNTAIN

My favorite way of thinking about this is to compare it with climbing a steep mountain. You can think of each different martial art as a different path to the summit.

There are many different trails to the top. Some are steeper and more direct, while others are gentler as they meander a little more. Some lead over rocky terrain while others cross the meadows. There is a right path for everyone.

The more different paths you take, the more different sides of the mountain you will expe-
rience. However, if you try out too many paths on the foothills and always flip between them, you will never reach any significant heights or get close to the summit.

Once you reach the summit, the view is the same. Everyone has the same experience, no matter the path they took.

That's why it's nonsense to talk about 'the best martial art'. There is no such thing. There are only different heights a specific practitioner has reached. It's all about the practitioner, not about the style.

Everyone who sticks to it until the top enjoys the same breathtaking views. However, you cannot describe the views in a meaningful way to others who haven't taken the climb, since the work to get there is part of the reward and experience. A glass of water is better when you're thirsty, a slice of bread tastes better when you're hungry. Without the work for it, you miss the flavor.

FIND YOUR OWN PATH

You cannot do that early on or you will get lost, but eventually, you need to find your own path. We all have the same physiology but we don't have exactly the same body. We also don't have the same way of thinking or experiencing the world. That's how different styles emerge. That's why practitioners will place different focus areas after a while and do things slightly different (if they don't, then they just copy someone else's approach without reflection).

Even for Uli and I, while we do the same Tai Chi, we learned the same arts on the way from the same teachers, we practice, explain and teach things slightly different. Uli is more focused on energy and imagination, while I often look closer to the martial arts roots and the body mechanics.

Like a beautiful vase, you can explain the colors and shapes or marvel at the static and balances. Or you can just focus on the smells of the flowers in the vase. The teacher shows one way of thinking about it, the student finds her own way through careful study over the years.

"If someone points to the moon – don't just look at the finger."
Buddha

THE LIFELONG APPRENTICE MINDSET

I was reading Mastery by Robert Green and one of the things that stuck out for me was how Robert stressed the importance of the 'apprenticeship phase' before creativity and mastery can be reached. It reminded me of key lessons I learned early (and unconsciously) through martial arts practice.

However, reflecting a little more I would suggest the learning mindset should never change and what one should truly develop is a 'lifelong apprentice mindset'.

NEVER STOP LEARNING NEW AREAS

Everyone talks about lifelong learning today. Most people think about deepening their subject area exper- tise when they do. I think there is a bigger opportunity hidden in expand- ing into com- pletely new areas.

Robert Greene has some such exam- ples in his book as well, as he discusses people who went through mul- tiple different apprenticeships over the time of their life, finally merging those skills together to understand underlying principles better or to de- velop completely new areas.

The most compelling opportunity that learning new areas opens up is the fact that the spectrum of things you can do widens instead of shrinking. If your focus is on getting better and better at one single thing, you face a good chance of either that thing becoming obsolete in the future or someone else outcompeting you in that narrowly scoped area. If you learn to do many things well, then your horizon of opportunities keeps expanding through your life as you mix those abilities into new compelling portfolios.

I learned this in martial arts, studying diverse disciplines and with that enhancing my core style. Looking back it rubbed off on my approach to professional life as well, where over the years I pursued experiences in coding, marketing, business development, PR, product management and teaching.

LEARN TO LOVE PAIN AND FRUSTRATION

Robert Greene mentions this as well: you must learn to embrace and seek learning experiences that are painful and frustrating. If you don't focus on the things that are hardest for you (and thus most painful and frustrating), then you won't learn the traits of your trade that you are deficient in and will never truly master the area.

It's way too easy to focus on the easy wins and the things that you're good at. I am guilty of that too. However only playing to your strengths will prevent you from expanding the scope of your abilities. While leading to quicker wins in the short time, it will limit your ability to master an area long term since you will never close those capability gaps.

Martial arts teaches through pain, sweat, and tears. For good schools that's figuratively rather than literally (maybe with the exception of the sweat part). However, they make you constantly face your biggest challenges and learn to overcome them. I think the same is true for our professional development, only with the big difference that it's usually up to you to push yourself beyond your limits. Business often offers you an easy way out until the day when it's too late to change. You need to be pushing yourself.

PUTTING IT INTO PRACTICE

Never stop learning. Never think you 'know it'.

When you feel like you've reached a comfortable level in mastering an area, then it's time to disrupt yourself and move on to something entirely different.

Focus on learning the skills that are hard for you. You will learn the things that align with your strengths anyway. As to learning time, your knowledge gaps are what needs the most attention.

ON MARTIAL ARTS AND BUSINESS

I have three big passions in my life: family, martial arts and developing people and teams. While following each of those passions I learned that common principles apply and each of those has cross-pollinated the other areas heavily.

I've been doing martial arts for more than 25 years now. Here are some of my personal principles that came over from that area into my career toolbox. None of the following is breathtakingly net-new (yes, you can stop reading now if you were hoping for that) but it's a framework that helps to remember some key principles.

DO IT OR DON'T DO IT BUT DON'T DO IT HALF-HEARTED

Be in the moment

Being in the moment is a key principle in martial arts, Zen, and meditation. It's about fo-cusing on the now and not getting distracted by what has been or what might be in the future.

This is extremely powerful for being effective in business as well. Focus on the task at hand and nothing else. Turn off notifications, put away your phone, and hide your email inbox. And come back to enjoy those distractions once you've accomplished your task.

It's also super important as you interact with people. Listening skills are a highly valued skill today mostly because many people cannot focus on what the person sitting in front of them is trying to tell them. Stop playing with your phone or thinking about your smart answer that you will provide in response. Just listen to the person and show her that you do. Your partnership will improve tremendously!

It's all or nothing

In martial arts, if you engage you engage. No matter what the consequences are, you already decided that it is critical to engage. And you will pull it through.

I've learned that in business we're often too afraid of losing to really do what it takes to succeed. I was most successful when we had no kids, two incomes and I really didn't care whether I would lose my job over bold decisions.

I love my job and want to keep it and I need to feed a family now but I do try to remind myself that you need to be willing to lose (everything) in order to make the bold decisions that are required to be successful.

If you think it is important enough to do it, do it all the way. My teacher used to say "there is no being half pregnant".

THINGS CHANGE, DON'T MISS THE OPPORTUNITY

Stay flexible

Be smart though. Things will change as you move along. The initial plan that you want to badly follow through might not be appropriate anymore. Keep your focus on the goal but don't get stubborn on your execution plan.

In martial arts, your partner seldom tends to react the way you think she should have reacted. Stay flexible, stay on your toes, and shift your execution as your parameters change.

Avoid blind spots

In order to stay flexible, you need to first know what's going on and recognize if situations change. In martial arts, we talk a lot about tunnel vision, the effect where you focus so much on one partner that you don't even see the other one approaches you from behind.

Maintain 360-degree vision. Obviously, you need to stay on top of what's going on in your industry and area of expertise as well as the broader initiatives in your company.

But you should extend your 360-degree awareness beyond business opportunities to your relationship with people. Are you deeply tuned into how people inter-act with you and how they react to you? Are you making it a point to reflect on how you  appear to people, what your behavior and your style projects? Do you observe how team members perceive your posture and even your dress style when they interact with you (ie do you send the signal that you value them as a partner and thus care about the impression you make on them)? Do you behave in employee 1:1s the way you would in an interview or a board meeting?

Keep it simple

In martial arts, the final mastery is to leave out everything that is not necessary. Slow is smooth, smooth is fast. If you leave everything out that is not necessary then the remaining is 100% effective (and yes, no one ever gets there).

In your work, simplify to be able to adapt faster. Process and complexity keep creeping up. Entropy will finally win (so much I remember from my physics master) but your job in life is to fight it.

Keep the mindset to constantly improve what's needed but don't be afraid to cut the rest. Focus on a few things and do them right (reminder: by definition focus does mean you can't do everything).

IT'S A JOURNEY, NOT A DESTINATION

Always remember that you're in for the long run. You better make sure you make it all the way to the finish line and won't drop out before. In martial arts, if you make an impressive first move but then go down badly you won't get many cheers (or feel great about it afterward).

Be balanced

If you're the world's greatest jump kicker someday a fellow will come along and wrestle you to the mat. And if you never thought about wrestling before you will feel really miserable down there.

Keep up your motivation by following and nurturing your passions (and by making sure that you have more than one passion). Sometimes things will go awesome in one area but sometimes it might be bumpy – in those situations, it's great to have a second source to pull motivation and energy from. It's bad if the only thing that defined you goes through a slow patch.

Don't be a one trick pony, they get burned out quickly. Don't neglect the things that are important to you. Balance your time across work, relationships and hobbies. Have all three of them!

A healthy mind in a healthy body

There is a Latin proverb for that. But I didn't take Latin in school and better not pretend to have any such skills.

The concept is easy though: you kind of life in your body. Every day. That makes it your most important tool of all, please don't break it.

Get the sleep you need (find out how much that is and then be religious about it). Do sports. You don't have to run a marathon. Find out what works for you and build a habit around it.

And pace yourself! At times you have to outperform everyone else. And it feels great to do so! But then there needs to be a time where you turn it down a notch and recharge your batteries. Pace yourself to be ready when ready is required. Don't burn all your energy before the race actually starts. Take your long and short breaks.

Never stop being a student

In martial arts, you never stop being a student. In fact, once you stop learning you start losing. It should be just the same in life.

Be humble but aspirational and keep a learning mindset. Keep learning and keep stretching yourself, that's actually the most fun part of life!

If you draw a short and a long line on the ground there are two ways to make the long line shorter. Most people try to wash some away from the long line, to erase it. That's hard and messy and generally a lot of work which more often than not fails. A lot of competitive strategies work that way today where one competitor tries to throw rocks in the other ones way. A much easier way is actually to extend the short line. Invest in your abilities and leave the competition behind.

FINAL THOUGHT

In martial arts, once it's done it's done. You can learn from the many mistakes you just made but you can't change any of them anymore – they're out the door. You also don't wallow in the past since it's meaningless.

With that, I will finish the summary of lessons we taught and re-discovered together and will conclude the 'teaching part' of this book as well.

TO THOSE WHO HAVE FORGOTTEN MORE THAN WE WILL EVER LEARN

"When the student is ready, the teacher will appear."
Buddhist proverb

OUR TEACHERS

HILMAR FUCHS

Hilmar Fuchs has been our teacher from the beginning of our martial arts journey. He is the most amazing teacher and friend we have ever met and he ignited our passion for the martial arts.

Hilmar introduced us to the self-defense as well as the healing aspects of

martial arts. He also made us understand how martial arts principles really are life principles. Most importantly, he always reminds us to have a good laugh and keep alive the child within.

Hilmar is an 8th Dan Karate, Kobudo and Tai Chi master. He is a holistic medicine practitioner and a great life philosopher.

http://mh-health.com/

ROLAND HABERSETZER

Roland Habersetzer is one of Hilmar's teachers and has been a big influence during our time in Europe. He has provided great inspiration and insight into the martial side of the arts.

Roland Habersetzer is a 9th Dan Karate, Kobudo and Tai Chi master and the author of countless books on martial arts.

http://www.tengu.fr/

NOBUKO RELNICK

Nobuko Relnick has been Uli's teacher since 2009 and has been an amazing inspiration for her.

Nobuko received her first teacher's certificate from Sogetsu Ikebana Headquarters in Tokyo, Japan in 1966. Thirty years later, in 1996, she was awarded the highest teacher's certificate the "Riji rank". She was a member of the Ikebana International Tokyo Founding

Chapter from 1988 to 1998, when she moved to Woodinville, WA. Here she was president of Ikebana International's Seattle Chapter from 2001

to 2003 and following this, she was President of the Seattle Branch of Sogetsu Ikebana until 2016.

Shortly after moving to Washington State in 1998, Nobuko opened her Woodinville Sogetsu Studio to continue her art and offer her experience to others. She is presently also teaching at the Pottery Northwest Center and volunteers her teaching at the Cancer Lifeline to promote Ikebana as a healing art. Her arrangements can be frequently seen at SAM, where she volunteers too.

http://sogetsuikebana.com/

IMPORTANT INFLUENCES

TSUGUO SAKUMOTO

While we've only trained with him a for short (and intense) period, Tsuguo Sa-kumoto was instrumental in breaking us out of the constraints of Shotokan Karate and opening our eyes for the wider variety of Karate approaches. Tsuguo Sakumoto is a 9th Dan Karate master.

https://www.sakumoto-karate.academy/home

DAVID ANDREWS

David showed us how to extend our martial arts experience into the world of defensive shooting. His safety training with Fist and Firearm teaches an integrated approach to self-defense both in the home and out on the street. Unfortunately, he stopped teaching due to other obligations.

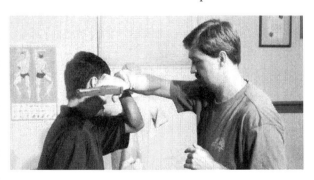

https://www.facebook.com/FistandFirearm/

THE PATH AHEAD

I t is said that in martial arts you develop along the path from student to fighter, from fighter to teacher, from teacher to healer and finally from healer to spiritual leader.

Our teacher, Hilmar Fuchs, has made the step into the spiritual leadership realm. We tipped our toes into being teachers.

As it was all the way along, we're curious to discover what lies ahead and where our paths will lead us.

Bodhidharma, Ukiyo-e woodblock print by Tsukioka Yoshitoshi, 1887

APPENDICES

"Empty your cup so that it may be filled. Become devoid to gain totality."
Bruce Lee

TAI CHI PRINCIPLES

Here is a list of basic principles that we emphasize in classes. Try to focus on one of them every time you practice. Over time they will become natural and you will be able to apply them without thinking.

I. **Principles of bow step** – Don't break your knees! Avoid tilt and torque.

II. **Focus on your eight points** – Always have firm contact to earth with at least 8 points. Be rooted.

III. **Cut the strings** – There is only one string left at the Bai Hui point (crown point), everything else drops. Everything above your neck rises, everything below drops.

IV. **Open and close** – Open and close your body like a flower in the morning and evening. Reach out to the universe and focus back in on your core.

V. **Empty and full** – Distinguish between empty and full. Have two containers and pump the water between them.

VI. **Tuck in your tailbone** – Lower your hips and tilt them forward. Tuck in your tailbone. Pretend that you are starting to sit down and then stop halfway into the movement.

VII. **Push from your Qi Hai and Ming Men points** – Push against resistance. Imagine to be in a pool and push against the water.

VIII. **Open your Lao Ghong and Yong Quan points** – Open and close your hands deliberately. Control and observe the energy flow. Don't trap the energy when you want to push.

IX. **Control your eyes** – Control your eyes and gaze. Don't be fixated but attentive (Zanshin) and mindful, ready to focus when needed.

X.   **Yin and Yang** – Keep moving, keep shifting. Never stop, never stagnate. Celebrate the black and white instead of perpetual grey.

XI.   **Qi follows Yi** – Energy follows intent.

IMPORTANT ACUPUNCTURE POINTS

Traditional Chinese medicine knows 2,000 acupuncture points on the human body, which are connected by 20 pathways (12 main, 8 secondary) called meridians. These meridians conduct energy, or Qi (氣), between the surface of the body and its internal organs.

In Tai Chi class we often refer to the following main points:

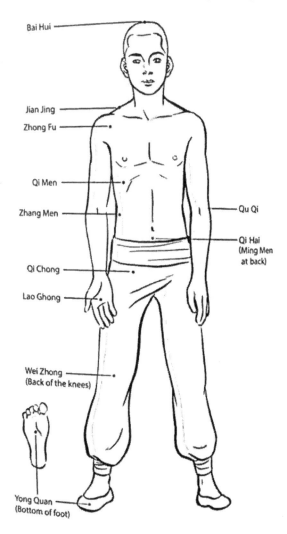

Specifically, remember the golden thread that pulls up your body from you Ba Hui point while everything else drops down.

Initiate all movements from your Dantien, pushing from your Qi Hai point when moving forward and pulling with your Ming Men point when shifting backward.

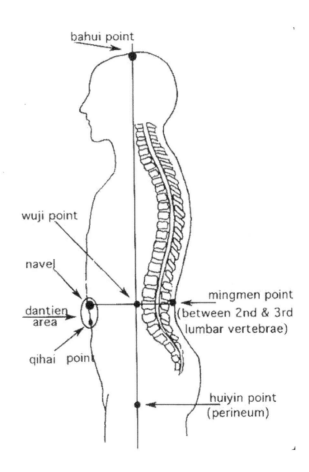

FORM OF 24

The movements of the Form of 24, also known as Beijing form.

The form of 24 is a beginner form that is relatively easy to learn and remember while offering the conduit to experience and learn all Tai Chi principles.

Always remember that the form is just a container. What matters is your working on, and understanding of the principles. And of course to have fun in what you're doing!

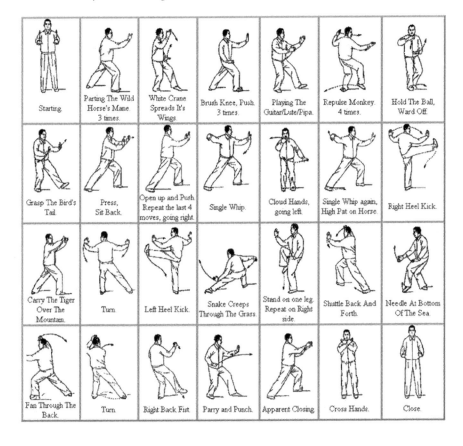

1. Commencing (Qǐ shì, 起势), Preparation, Beginning

2. Part the Wild Horse's Mane (Zuoyou Yémǎ Fēnzōng, **左右野马分鬃**), LEFT and RIGHT

3. White Crane Spreads Its Wings (Báihè Liàngchì, **白鹤亮翅**), Stork/Crane Cools Its Wings

4. Brush Knee and Step Forward (Zuoyou Lōuxī Àobù, **左右搂膝拗步**), Brush Knee and Twist Step, LEFT and RIGHT

5. Playing the Lute (Shǒuhūi Pípā, **手挥琵琶**), Strum the Lute, Play Guitar

6. Reverse Reeling Forearm (Zuoyou Dào juǎn gōng, **左右倒卷肱**), Step Back and Repulse Monkey (Dǎo niǎn hóu **倒攆猴**), LEFT and RIGHT

7. Left Grasp Sparrow's Tail (Zuo Lǎn Què Wěi, **左**揽雀尾), Grasp the Bird's Tail

a. Ward Off (Peng, **掤**)

b. Rollback (Lǚ, **捋**)

c. Press (Jǐ, **挤**)

d. Push (Àn, **按**)

8. Right Grasp Sparrow's Tail (You Lǎn què wěi, **右揽雀尾**)

9. Single Whip (Dān biān, 单鞭)

10. Wave Hands Like Clouds (Yúnshǒu, **云手**), Cloud Hands, Cloud Built Hands, Wave Hands in Clouds

11. Single Whip (Dan biān, 单鞭)

12. High Pat on Horse (Gāo tàn mǎ , 高探马), Step Up to Examine Horse

13. Right Heel Kick (Yòu dēng jiǎ o, 右蹬脚), Separate Right Foot, Kick with Right Foot

14. Strike to Ears with Both Fists (Shuāng fēng guàn ěr, 双峰贯耳)

15. Turn Body and Left Heel Kick (Zhuǎ nshēn zuǒ dēngjiǎ o, 转身左蹬脚)

16. Left Lower Body and Stand on One Leg (Zuo Xià shì dúlì, 左下势独立)
    a.   Single Whip Squatting Down, Snake Creeps Down,
    b.   Golden Rooster Stands on One Leg

17. Right Lower Body and Stand on One Leg (You Xià shì dúlì, 右下势独立)

18. Shuttle Back and Forth (Yòuzuǒ yùnǚ chuānsuō, 右左玉女穿梭), Fair Lady Works with Shuttles, (Walking Wood), Four Corners, RIGHT and LEFT

19. Needle at Sea Bottom (Hǎ idǐ zhēn, 海底针)

20. Fan Through Back (Shǎ n tōng bì, 闪通臂), Fan Penetrates Back

21. Turn Body, Deflect, Parry, and Punch (Zhuǎ nshēn Bānlánchuí, 转身搬拦捶)

22. Appears Closed (Rúfēng shìbì, 如封似闭), Withdraw and Push, as if Closing a Door

23. Cross Hands (Shízìshǒ u, 十字手)

24. Closing (Shōushì, 收势)

FORM OF 103 – YANG FORM

The Yang form is the second form that we are typically learning. It is divided into three sections, Earth, Human and Heaven, and usually takes a year to get through the basics.

After that it takes a lifetime to learn and master. Like everything in Tai Chi.

第一段 | EARTH, SECTION 1

1. 预备 | Yùbèi | Preparation Form

2. 起式 | Qǐ shì | Beginning

3. 揽雀尾 | Lǎn què wěi | Grasp the Bird's tail

4. 单鞭 | Dān biān | Single Whip

5. 提手上势 | Tí shǒu shàng shì | Raise Hands and Step Forward

6. 白鹤亮翅 | Bái hè liàng chì | White Crane Spreads its Wings

7. 左搂膝拗步 | Zuǒ lōu xǐǎo bù | Left Brush Knee and Push

8. 手挥琵琶 | Shǒu huī pípá | Hand Strums the Lute

9. 左搂膝拗步 | Zuǒ lōu xǐǎo bù | Left Brush Knee and Push

10. 右搂膝拗步 | Yòu lōu xǐǎo bù | Right Brush Knee and Push

11. 左搂膝拗步 | Zuǒ lōu xǐǎo bù | Left Brush Knee and Push

12. 手挥琵琶 | Shǒu huī pípá | Hand Strums the Lute

13. 左搂膝拗步 | Zuǒ lōu xǐǎo bù | Left Brush Knee and Push

14. 进步搬拦捶 | Jìn bù bān lán chuí | Step Forward, Parry, Block, and Punch

15. 如封似闭 | Rú fēng shì bì | Apparent Close Up

16. 十字手 | Shí zì shǒ u | Cross Hands

17. **抱虎归山** | Bào hǔ guī shān | Embrace the Tiger and Return to Mountain

18. **肘底捶** | Zhǒu dǐ chuí | Fist Under Elbow

19. **左倒撵猴** | Zuǒ dào niǎn hóu | Step Back and Repulse the Monkey, Left

20. **右倒撵猴** | Yòu dào niǎn hóu | Step Back and Repulse the Monkey, Right

21. **左倒撵猴** | Zuǒ dào niǎn hóu | Step Back and Repulse the Monkey, Left

22. **斜飞式** | Xié fēi shì | Diagonal Flying

23. **提手上势** | Tí shǒu shàng shì | Raise Hands and Step Forward

24. **白鹤亮翅** | Bái hè liàng chì | White Crane Spreads its Wings

25. **左搂膝拗步** | Zuǒ lōu xiǎo bù | Left Brush Knee and Push

26. **海底针** | Hǎi dǐ zhēn | Needle at Sea Bottom

27. **扇通背** | Shàn tōng bèi | Fan Through the Back

28. **转身撇身捶** | Zhuǎn shēn piē shēn chuí | Turn Body and Chop with Fist

29. **进步搬拦捶** | Jìn bù bān lán chuí | Step Forward, Parry, Block, and Punch

30. **上步揽雀尾** | Shàng bù lǎn què wěi | Step Forward and Grasp the Bird's Tail

31. 单鞭 | Dān biān | Single Whip

32. 云手 | Yún shǒu | Cloud Hands (1)

33. 云手' | Yún shǒu | Cloud Hands (2)

34. 云手 | Yún shǒu | Cloud Hands (3)

35. 单鞭 | Dān biān | Single Whip

36. 高探马 | Gāo tàn mǎ | High Pat on Horse

37. 右分脚 | Yòu fēn jiǎo | Right Separation Kick

38. 左分脚 | Zuǒ fèn jiǎo | Left Separation Kick

39. 转身左蹬脚 | Zhuǎn shēn zuǒ dēng jiǎo | Turn Body and Left Heel Kick

40. 左搂膝拗步 | Zuǒ lōu xī ǎo bù | Left Brush Knee and Push

41. 右搂膝拗步 | Yòu lōu xī ǎo bù | Right Brush Knee and Push

42. 进步栽锤 | Jìn bù zāi chuí | Step Forward and Punch Down

43. 转身撇身锤 | Zhuǎn shēn piē shēn chuí | Turn Body and Chop with Fist

44. 进步搬拦锤 | Jìn bù bān lán chuí | Step Forward, Parry, Block, and Punch

45. 右蹬脚 | Yòu dēng jiǎo | Right Heel Kick

46. 左打虎式 | Zuǒ dǎ hǔ shì | Left Strike Tiger

47. 右打虎式 | Yòu dǎ hǔ shì | Right Strike Tiger

48. **回身右蹬脚** | Huí shēn yòu dēng jiǎo | Turn Body and Right Heel Kick

49. **双峰灌耳** | Shuāng fēng guàn ěr | Twin Fists Strike Opponents Ears

50. **左蹬脚** | Zuǒ dēng jiǎo | Left Heel Kick

51. **转身右蹬脚** | Zhuǎn shēn yòu dēng jiǎo | Turn Body and Right Heel Kick

52. **进步搬拦锤** | Jìn bù bān lán chuí | Step Forward, Parry, Block, and Punch

53. **如封似闭** | Rú fēng shì bì | Apparent Close Up

54. **十字手** | Shí zì shǒu | Cross Hands

55. **抱虎**归山 | Bào hǔ guī shān | Embrace the Tiger and Return to Mountain

56. **斜**单鞭 | Xié dān biān | Diagonal Single Whip

57. **右野**马分鬃 | Yòu yě mǎ fēn zōng | Parting Wild Horse's Mane, Right

58. **左野**马分鬃 | Zuǒ yě mǎ fēn zōng | Parting Wild Horse's Mane, Left

59. **右野**马分鬃 | Yòu yě mǎ fēn zōng | Parting Wild Horse's Mane, Right

60. 揽雀尾 | Lǎ n què wěi | Grasp the Bird's tail

61. 单鞭 | Dān biān | Single Whip

62. **玉女穿梭** | Yù nǚ chuān suō | Fair Lady Works at Shuttles

63. 揽雀尾 | Lǎ n què wěi | Grasp the Bird's tail

64. 单鞭 | Dān biān | Single Whip

65. **云手** | Yún shǒ u | Cloud Hands (1)

66. **云手** | Yún shǒ u | Cloud Hands (2)

67. **云手** | Yún shǒ u | Cloud Hands (3)

68. 单鞭 | Dān biān | Single Whip

69. **下势** | Xià shì | Snake Creeps Down

70. **左**金鸡独立 | Zuǒ jīn jī dú lì | Golden Rooster Stands on One Leg, Left

71. **右**金鸡独立 | Yòu jīn jī dú lì | Golden Rooster Stands on One Leg, Right

72. **左**倒撵猴 | Zuǒ dào niǎn hóu | Step Back and Repulse the Monkey, Left

73. **右**倒撵猴 | Yòu dào niǎn hóu | Step Back and Repulse the Monkey, Right

74. **左**倒撵猴 | Zuǒ dào niǎn hóu | Step Back and Repulse the Monkey, Left

75. **斜**飞势 | Xié fēi shì | Diagonal Flying

76. **提手上势** | Tí shǒu shàng shì | Raise Hands and Step Forward

77. **白鹤亮翅** | Bái hè liàng chì | White Crane Spreads its Wings

78. **左**搂膝拗步 | Zuǒ lōu xiǎo bù | Left Brush Knee and Push

79. **海底针** | Hǎi dǐ zhēn | Needle at Sea Bottom

80. **扇通背** | Shàn tōng bèi | Fan Through the Back

81. 转身白蛇吐信 | Zhuǎn shēn bái shé tǔ xìn | Turn Body and White Snake Spits out Tongue

82. 进步搬拦捶 | Jìn bù bān lán chuí | Step Forward, Parry, Block, and Punch

83. **上步**揽雀尾 | Shàng bù lǎn què wěi | Step Forward and Grasp the Bird's tail

84. 单鞭 | Dān biān | Single Whip

85. 云手 | Yún shǒu | Cloud Hands (1)

86. 云手 | Yún shǒu | Cloud Hands (2)

87. 云手 | Yún shǒu | Cloud Hands (3)

88. 单鞭 | Dān biān | Single Whip

89. 高探马穿掌 | Gāo tàn mǎ chuān zhǎng | High Pat On Horse with Palm Thrust

90. 十字腿 | Shí zì tuǐ | Cross Kick

91. 进步指裆锤 | Jìn bù zhǐ dāng chuí | Step Forward and Punch Groin

92. 上步揽雀尾 | Shàng bù lǎn què wěi | Step Forward and Grasp the Bird's tail

93. 单鞭 | Dān biān | Single Whip

94. 下势 | Xià shì | Snake Creeps Down

95. 上步七星 | Shàng bù qī xīng | Step Forward Seven Stars

96. 退步跨虎 | Tuì bù kuà hǔ | Step back and Ride the Tiger

97. 转身摆莲 | Zhuǎn shēn bǎi lián | Turn Body and Swing Over Lotus

98. 弯弓射虎 | Wān gōng shè hǔ | Bend the Bow and Shoot the Tiger

99. 进步搬拦捶 | Jìn bù bān lán chuí | Step Forward, Parry, Block, and Punch

100. 如封似闭 | Rú fēng shì bì | Apparent Close Up

101. 十字手 | Shí zì shǒu | Cross Hands

102. **收式** | Shōu shì | Closing

103. **还原** | Huán yuán | Return to Normal

Yang Chengfu in the Single Whip posture

BOOK RECOMMENDATIONS

TAI CHI

Der Tanz des Kranichs by Hilmar Fuchs
Palisander Verlag, First edition (July 20, 2015)
ISBN-10: 3938305835

Laoshi: Tai Chi, Teachers, and Pursuit of Principle by Jan Kauskas
Via Media Publishing; First edition (May 2, 2014)
ISBN-10: 0615967361

Tai Chi - The Perfect Exercise by Arthur Rosenfeld
Da Capo Lifelong Books; First edition (June 4, 2013)
ISBN-10: 0738216607

MARTIAL ARTS

Zen in the Martial Arts by Joe Hyams
J. P. Tarcher Inc./Houghton Mifflin Company; New edition (October 1, 1979)
ISBN-10: 0874771013

The Art of Peace: Teachings of the Founder of Aikido by Morihei Ueshiba
Shambhala; 1st edition (November 10, 1992)
ISBN-10: 0877738513

Karate-Do: My Way of Life by Gichin Funakoshi
Kodansha International; Reprint edition (February 1, 2013)
ISBN-10: 1568364989

RELATED SCIENCE

Peak by Anders Ericsson
Eamon Dolan/Mariner Books; Reprint edition (April 11, 2017)
ISBN-10: 0544947223

Presence by Amy Cuddy
Little, Brown and Company; First edition (December 22, 2015)
ISBN-10: 0316256579

Mastery by Robert Greene
Penguin Books; Reprint edition (October 29, 2013)
ISBN-10: 014312417X

In Closing

Thank you for reading this book and following our thoughts.

We would love to hear from you! You can send us a message through our website www.KeruUmaBudo.com or sign up for our mailing list from there. You can follow our blog on KeruUmaBudo.wordpress.com.

Consider leaving a review on Amazon. Share if you liked the book, let us know how we can improve if you didn't.

Join a class if you are in the area. Most important: Keep practicing, have fun and enjoy the ride!

Made in the USA
San Bernardino, CA
30 November 2018